OUR LADY OF THE FOREST

Our Lady
of the
Forest

A BOOK OF MARY NAMES

SISTER MARY JULIAN BAIRD, R.S.M.

THE BRUCE PUBLISHING COMPANY
MILWAUKEE

NIHIL OBSTAT:

JOANNES A. SCHULIEN, S.T.D.
Censor librorum

IMPRIMATUR:

✠ ALBERTUS G. MEYER
Archiepiscopus Milwauchiensis

March 5, 1957

Rosary College Dewey Classification Number: 232.931

Library of Congress Catalog Card Number: 57–9130

DEDICATED TO

MARY, OUR MOTHER

CONTENTS

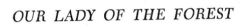

OUR LADY OF THE FOREST

INTRODUCTION: *OUR LADY OF THE FOREST*

LIGHT darkens suddenly as evening falls in the deep woods. Simultaneously with the graying of the sky begin the soft night noises. Such slight stirrings are touching in their hint of small furry folks settling to rest, but alarming to us who have forgotten our way out of the forest.

All others seek repose. In the gathering gloom, we must find our way out of this black theater of sleep. We must escape a growing unrest beneath the blanketing dusk, for there are powers that work only in the darkness now upon us. O swift and savage wing darting down above the roof of trees! O stealthy padded step not far behind us!

Can this be the fairyland through which we sauntered blithely in the late afternoon? A low sun-flecked green sea of foliage. Bright bird song caroled. There was laughter in every golden cloud, and in our hearts. As bells pealed from distant towers we said the *Angelus*, that chant of praise to her who is Queen of Heaven. Our sole petition to her was for grace to match with the loveliness of prayer the magic beauty of the woodlands.

Now we cry to her in stricken silence. Who would dare to risk a call louder than a heartbeat in this land of furtive fear? We repeat one word, one muted plea powerful enough to reach beyond peril to the gates of peace. "Mother," we say again and again. "Mother!"

This is the name she longs to hear. When in primitive fear we have laid aside pride and called that name, she comes to us, swift through the shadows, a Woman clad in light, and on her brow the star of love undying. BEHOLD THY MOTHER.

A HEAP of gold they have laid at her feet, the fruit of meadows full of dandelions. Hundreds of golden heads pulled free by childish hands and brought to her in tribute now wilt to sullen yellow on the grass around her where children are sleeping in the mellow sun. Their day's work must please them, for they smile in slumber.

She watches them quietly. In a few weeks they will bring her other gifts. Carefully holding gray-beard flowers gone to seed, they will run joyously across the same field, clamoring, "Mother, what time is it?"

"What time indeed? Blow the dandelion clock, small one. One puff! All seeds gone? One o'clock! Two puffs. Two o'clock! Three . . . But wait. Mother will help you. Together. There, it is only three o'clock, and we need not go home until five. Run off and play some more."

So shall it be in all little lives. "Mother, what time is it? Must we go home yet?" And she will comfort them. Out of this weed's decay, she will fashion truth. Not time yet to go. Not time now to leave the joy that you think lasting. A little while, child, for sun and careless pleasure. What time is it? Blow, blow the tiny trumpet of your breath and make the seeds of golden happiness spin on the breeze of summer. Let them lie close entombed in earth until another year when other children will romp this meadow. You will not care then. You will learn another way to tell time. Slowly. Slowly. Children cannot learn too quickly. Poor little heads ache soon enough with tedious problems.

What time is it, Mother? Still time to play, my little one. Still time to sleep at the feet of one who loves you and cares for you. Sleep, for Mother is here.

≫ 1 ≪

OUR LADY

OF

CLOCKS

PROUDLY they watch her, their Mother, in the court of the King. They know there is no one so beautifully regal as she. No one so perfect a Queen. Shyly they touch the gold of her jeweled gown, the bracelets, the shining rings. But they dare not climb upon the sheen of that gown to lay hesitant fingers on the gleaming crown on her dusky hair. With all the rest of her loyal subjects they bow as she rises from the throne, as she glides past them among her royal attendants, leaning on the arm of the King.

If it were always so, how unhappy those little hearts would be. At nightfall, framed in the nursery door, how strange to see this splendor. Were she Queen always, how could she be Mother too?

"Lay down the dainty crown, Queen-Mother. Strip off rings, jagged with gems in exotic settings. Loose the heavy cloak with its hard metal brooch upon your breast. Take off the silken dress that small hands might snag, and put on the woolen robe they know so well. Come then, soft hair curling on your shoulders, simple as any peasant girl. Stand now in the doorway, and our hearts leap with joy. It is our Mother who comes, not in pomp and finery, not for strangers and statesmen. Only for us she comes tonight, to bend above our cribs and lift us to her heart for a tender caress.

"Arms strong in love to lift us. Loving heart to which our heads are pressed. Sweet hair, falling a fragrant curtain about our faces, a secrecy for her gentle kiss. This is our Mother's good night.

"Be Queen for the King. Queen for the court. Queen for the world. But for us, O Mary, be to us only our Mother always."

2

SILENCE sings in the valley but on the hills there are echoes. It is the children's paradise of melody. Small voices ring harsh in the valley, but here they shrink to elfin horns.

Only one word is echoed on the plateau of the love of Mary. "MARIA!" the children call, over and over. At morning it is a golden word, and its echo more gentle than the dew on the rose of dawning. The sound summons, but softly. There is no commanding in the echo of the name of Mary.

The cry in the morning is all acclaim, all praise, all exultation. *"Ave, Maria!"* Gabriel once greeted her, and the name has echoed since in all the mornings of the world. "Hail," says the word of morning. "Thou art all fair, O Mary, and there is no stain of Adam's sin in thee." Light shines from the echo in the fresh, crystal air. Light lives in the echo of its echo. On, on through the day it lingers, so that no one need call again until the night comes on.

But at evening — purple evening stealing down across the meadows — the children's voices call again, "MARIA!" It is a different echo now, even as it is a different cry. Night is coming. "Thanks, Mother, for the joy of the day. Come now to us with evening. Be thou our evening star, more silver against the blue velvet of the sky than golden at morning. Shine on our dreams, MARIA. While you bend over us, there is no fear. MARIA!" The echo rings back with a tender note. In it is less than triumph, more than tears. With the wistful sweep of the night wind, it colors the world with hope. Sing out once more, children, that dear name. MARIA! Then a *good* night, for Mary guards.

SHALL we be unmindful of our Mother's tears?

Who can watch, unmoved, the queenly figure seated on the mountain, her lovely face hidden in her hands, her tears a silver fountain?

Why should a queen weep? Because she is a mother. She is a queen because she is a mother. She is a mother before she is a queen.

What makes her weep? The sins that killed her Jesus.

Why does she not seize the rays so brilliant from the crown upon her head to cast like bolts of lightning upon the sinning world? But that might harm her children!

Do not her children need sometimes to be chastized? How else shall they realize the evil that they do?

When the stream of her sorrow floods their souls with grief for their sins, then they will understand. When the murmur of the fountain of her tears rises above the thunder of their blatant ego, they will remember her.

Hear then their feet upon the mountain. See her rise and reach out hands to those who come, themselves now weeping, to comfort her.

"Lady of lucent tears," they will say, "weep no longer, for we come to thee. Out of the desert of our selfish hearts, we seek the fountain of repentance. And in thy peace we shall find the garden of repose."

Let then the queen weep quietly. Sunrise and starrise on the mountain will find her there.

But not alone. Softly her few faithful children will creep to her side, slip small hands into hers. For the golden joy she has given them, they return the silver music of their tears. So shall they comfort her.

A BIRD flies into the church during the children's Mass. Into the night of a church from the bright morning sunshine comes a wandering robin, attracted to the new world where stars gleam in a heaven of flowers and brilliant music bursts from a vast organ.

The older children sing on, unconcerned as the bewildered visitor swoops overhead. But the small ones rise in a soft storm of glee, waving hands to follow his swift flight. Up and up he flashes, to light a moment on the Madonna's crown. Then down again, and back and forth, in frenzied fear.

The mystery of the Mass is forgotten in the magic of this aerial dance. With the bird's rhythm, small bodies sway until he finds escape through the same window that he entered. Back to the out-of-doors he flees. Joy for him lies in the freedom of trees and the boundless sunlight.

The Mass moves on. Chastened by the bell of the *Sanctus,* the small ones kneel. Only a fair-haired little boy dreamily waves arms as if the bird were still in flight.

Wee child of Mary, she will not frown on him or on the hapless robin. High winds bend strong saplings, but they do not break. Back to the blue sky they spring with release of pressure. The consecration bell will win the child's attention back to God. The same hand that followed the bird's dances waves now at the golden chalice raised to the golden cross. This is the child's world as the sky is the bird's. Here is his freedom and his love. Our Lady of Lost Birds and of Little Ones will give to each his ultimate joy.

⋈ 5 ⋊

OUR LADY
OF THE
LOST BIRD

HERS is the beautiful face that haloes His head for always. The setting of her loveliness shows off the Heart of Light. Within the lunette of her arms she cradles Him, till time to show Him to the world of men. Then it is her hands that lift Him slowly, the Christ Child, the Host-Child. She is the monstrance of Jesus.

About the little face of Jesus at Bethlehem is a glow, a nimbus in the smile of Mary, His Mother. Against her radiance blooms the single Rose of Christ. Angels and shepherds and kings bow down before her, where earlier only a carpenter knelt. She that was His tabernacle is now His ostensorium. Glorious choirs sing. The little King would bless His people from the arms of her who is His throne.

⊱ 6 ⊰

HALO OF THE HOST

Hers is the beautiful face that haloes His head for always, even when Calvary's dark curtain would conceal His shame. They think that He is dead and turn away, for He is terrible to look upon, beaten and bruised, far beyond desire or delight. But her luminous face shines unshadowed above His battered beauty. He is her Rose still, though crushed and torn. He is her God still, though dethroned in death.

Hers is the beautiful face that haloes His head at Easter, that head uncrowned of thorns and hallowed by the wonder of her joy that kisses the soft hair where once dark blood clung pitifully. Her eyes the Easter dawn. Her heart the garden in which His victory blooms.

Soft old gold and deep-hued gems in a delicate filigree frame forever her Jesus in the monstrance that is His Mother's love. Sing, angels, "O come, let us adore!"

Down the long corridor of hours I hear the sweet-toned bell of Mary's voice. Through the night of pain I dreamed its music, bringing me Jesus. And now He comes. I can believe her word. She never deceives. More than St. John the Baptist, she is the precursor of our Lord, for her *Ecce Ancilla Domini* preceded and made possible his *Ecce Agnus Dei*.

Closer the muffled bell, and with it I can hear swishing robes, swift feet of him who bears God in his hands. How shall I receive this visit of the Almighty?

"Acolyte of Jesus, my Mother Mary, stand beside Him at the threshold. Silence completely the bell and shade the too brilliant candle in your hand. Enter with Him this room where death has battled, where dark visions still stain soft-tinted walls. Conquer them by thy power, Immaculate Queen. Cleanse the thoughts of a mind, the love of a heart that longs to welcome the God of Purity and Peace."

"I confess to almighty God, to Blessed Mary ever Virgin. . . . Pray to the Lord our God for me. May the almighty and merciful Lord grant me pardon, absolution, and remission of all my sins. . . ."

"Hold now the candle high, Mother, that I may see Him who is the Lamb of God. My eyes are washed from sin and slothful negligence. He will come then, even to me."

"May the Body of our Lord Jesus Christ preserve thy soul. . . ."

"*Amen*, Mother. So be it. Put aside candle and bell to kneel beside my bed as at Bethlehem, as at Calvary, as in the Easter garden. It is your Jesus who dwells in me. Love Him for me, Mother. Praise, thank, adore. *Amen. Amen.*"

THE King shall walk in beauty. Before Him, on the feast of Corpus Christi, will be spread the color and perfume of countless gardens. Soft petals gathered from the sunny fields before sunrise lie now upon the road in varied patterns, for this day He shall pass in triumph among His own.

One street shall be more blessed by Him than any other — the street of Mary. Here there are fifteen separate pictures painted out in rare rose leaves, all the mysteries of His life and hers.

The innocence of white rose petals lies eloquent against the blue of larkspur. It is the Dove of the Annunciation. And spelled in letters of gold, the word MAGNIFICAT! Crimson leaves for angels' wings proclaim His birth, and for His Presentation, bright-petaled candle flames.

Will He not walk with joy this pathway of remembrance? How happy feet that tread the sweetness of this road! If there is pain through the sorrowful mysteries, it is pain fragrant with peace, purple petals redolent with love.

But glory — how can even flowers match the heavenly mysteries? The sweetness of the air that Easter morning, the white cloud that hid Him from their sight on the mount of the Ascension, the fire and wind of Pentecost. Lightly they lie upon the road, these ethereal reminders, and her own bright crown traced in sunset hues.

The King shall walk in beauty here, today and every day. For on the Street of Mary it is always Corpus Christi. Never does she forget His abiding Presence. Wherever He walks, she spreads before His feet her remembering love. He shall walk in eternal beauty in her heart.

8

"I WILL go to the altar of God, to God who gives joy to my youth," our Lady begins her Mass. The joy that God has given to her youth is her Jesus. The altar to which she goes, led often by strange ways, is the high altar of the will of God.

Somber, sometimes, is the chant for that Mass of Mary, lighted by the dark, prophetic candles of Simeon as well as by the jubilant faith of Elizabeth. If all heaven sings her *Gloria*, yet all earth bows with her — a child of earth bearing the Son of Man — for a profound *Confiteor*.

Others read the Gospel. Mary lives it. When knees bend during the Creed, for the sacred words of the Incarnation, Mary stands, her head bowed, her beautiful hands folded on her heart, and prays silently her *Magnificat*.

At the Offertory it is her virgin hands that raise the paten and the chalice to the Father, beseeching pity for the world of souls that needs it so. For them alone she washes spotless fingers. For them she pleads, as long ago at Cana.

For all she lifts up hands again in gratitude, since "it is fitting that we give thanks to Thee, Father Almighty — at all times, in all places."

Silence falls, as on the hidden life of Jesus, only to be shattered by the bell of Consecration, which signals the death of God and His eternal resurrection. Softly Mary prays through a deeper silence, for peace, for bread, and turns once more to the Cenacle where the Eucharist began.

When her children have received her Jesus, she dismisses them gently. "Go, the Mass is ended," she counsels but calls them back to repeat John's glorious words, lest they forget that Jesus is life and light.

SHE is the star for which the new kings watch — the Woman of their prophecies. Hidden now more deeply than before, how shall He be discovered by those who are too weary to search? Harder to find now because they say, "We have looked there before and found Him not. Christianity is for the worldly West."

Yet will they heed her, His Blessed Mother. Light rises from the dawn that is a Woman's face. Let her quiet love shine on above their ancient lands. Egypt of old saw her pass, bearing Jesus, and did not recognize Him or her. Two thousand years find still a hidden God, and pointing to Him still the Star of Mary.

This is the lamp that hangs over the Sacrament of Love unendingly. Where there is Jesus, there is always Mary. She adores, she repairs, she watches. Hers is the faithful heart that never leaves Him.

Some day they will find her, the seeking ones. Beyond the border of forgotten worlds, they will discover that steadfast Star. In God's providential plan the day will come when those "other sheep" will come to pastures long deserted, and Mary will be their shepherdess. Slow to learn, like underprivileged children, they will be swift too in love.

Will she weary of their waiting more than she wearies of our long forgetting? We have neglected what we should have loved and cherished — yes, and shared. But they are waiting for they know not what. Eyes on the night sky, they watch for the sign to say that their King has come. When they find the star of Mary, they will follow to the hidden God, to the home that her heart has guarded for them, to which it will lead them at last.

❧ 10 ❦
STAR
OF THE
EUCHARIST

THE crown of thorns of our sins lay in our Lady's lap. They are not her thorns any more than they were Jesus', yet she holds them preciously. These are the price of the peace of the world.

Peace of mind is dear in a world that lacks her wisdom. "To whom shall we go?" modern Peters ask, not knowing the answer as did the fisherman of the Gospel. To know in sure faith that Christ Crucified is the Son of the Living God — this certainly is bought by the nagging thorns that lie now in her compassionate hands.

His are the torturing questionings. Upon His eyes falls the curtain of blood that Veronica would wipe away as only love can heal the blindness of other Christs who walk, even unwittingly, the Way of His Cross.

⊁ 11 ⊱

OUR LADY
OF
THORNS

Love is the answer too to the tender care with which our Lady handles these sharp branches twined in cruelty and worn in pain. Yet Love wove the crown, even with the hands of hate. Love wore the crown, even unto death. Love then loosed the crown and looks with love upon it.

It is love that is the fulfilling of every law, but especially love that compassionates. Salvation lies in pity. Only the heart that pities can save. And only the heart that pities can be saved. There is no place in heaven for those who do not care for others, who will not look with understanding pity upon those who fear and fall. If we must ourselves fail to pity failure, then may God make us fail.

The heart of Mary did not need this lesson. That heart was made to love. She has but to look to have pity.

Lady of Thorns, teach us the pity of thy most tender heart.

EVERYTHING died on Calvary that day, even the light of God. But in the darkness one beauty glowed, deathless and dear, the Rose that was Mary.

This is the beauty that is love, the heart of goodness, the core of life. Into its radiance it draws all darkness. Out of the darkness, it perfects peace.

Upon the blackened mountain blossomed the Rose of the Cross. Exquisite and flawless, petal within petal unfolded as the night closed in and Jesus died. For sin was the cloud that shut out the sun, and she alone was sinless. Hate was the heart of sin and she was love.

Here at His feet forever blooms the Rose that is His Mother's beauty. Up to His dead face she lifts the perfume of her immaculate love. Into His dead eyes shine the tender light of her faithful devotion.

She is the one flower in the world that cannot die. Her loyal love is always. Those who climb that hill, for love or hate, will find her there, rooted and changeless, until time becomes eternity. Crimson the Rose to those who love; pure white to those who repent. But to those who come in hate it shows an ebony beauty. For them it is a black Rose, perfect in form but dark and dimmed. They cannot break the fact of love, but they can rob it, in their own eyes, of luster. If they can find strength to bend and kiss the feet of the dead Crucified, its light will spring forth for them. Upon the midnight petals will rush the crimson blood of love and in its heart will burn the brightness of her gladness. The Rose of death will become, for them too, the Rose of life.

❧ 12 ❦
ROSE
OF THE
CROSS

IMPETUOUSLY, through a strangely narrow path, for a brief ten minutes, tore a giant wind. Trees generations old were rooted up and thrown down. One huge trunk slashed off the arm of the bronze crucifix in the convent garden. Cruelty again struck the Christ.

They took Him down and laid Him on the ground amid the universal wreckage. In all that scene of desolation, His was the only tranquil face. For He was a gentle Jesus. His face was no longer tortured with pain beyond human conjecture. He was peaceful in death.

So Mary, His Mother, must have knelt beside Him, looked at that beloved face, and kissed Him in grateful love. The worst that sin could do, she must have thought, was over.

"Sleep sweetly, Saviour of the world, my Jesus. Thy task is done. And soon Thou shalt wake to glory."

Carpenters will make the garden Christ another cross, the Christ of the hurricane. Artists will mend His broken arm and bronze Him again to beauty. Other autumns will crown Him with woodland glory. New trees will shade Him from summer suns. But to those who saw Him, broken and prone upon the ground, there will be always the memory of her spirit coming with the wild storms of late winter and early spring, like a great wind of love to wrest Him from the cross and lay Him in peace in the garden.

Shall we let Him rest there, ignored and forsaken? Shall we let Mary kneel alone beside the still Figure? With the sun grown warm with increasing spring, with the birds back from the south, with the flowers weaving their colors through the green undergrowth, let us stay with her. From the fierceness of storm she will teach the peace of the Crucified.

JESUS might have asked her to be the mother of men during His childhood. John the Baptist, playing at His side, might have been the John to symbolize the whole human race. One slight gesture from His baby hand to say: "Behold thy son," and Mary would have remembered.

Or after the Resurrection, before the Ascension, it might have been easier for her to accept a substitute for her Son and God's. As Jesus raised His hands in final blessing, He might have said: "Behold thy mother." And all who gathered at that mountain would have welcomed her as His parting gift to them.

Calvary — Calvary — why did it have to be Calvary? Had she not enough to bear in watching Him die? Like Eve confronted by Cain after the murder of Abel, his brother's blood still staining his hands, Mary could well have drawn back even from the innocent John. They were all, sons of Adam, guilty of this brutal murder.

But she did not. This was the sword of sorrow in her heart. Children of her own she would make of these sons of men, in bitter pain. "Mother them for me," her Jesus would ask, and she would do His will. Here lies the Passion of Mary. It is her own who have killed her Own. They have desolated her heart with His. Yet she will forgive and love them still.

Mother of the Redeemed, even before the Redemption, her heart is close enough to the Heart of Jesus to share His forgiving love. With His divine magnanimity, she can behold all sinners and call them her sons. And because of this, sinners through the ages can call the Mother of God their mother.

≫ 14 ≪

MOTHER

OF

ALL MEN

DISMAS looked down. From the height of his cross he saw a circle of faces frozen in hate. He closed his eyes.

What did it matter? Soon he would be dead. And death was the end. Life had not been so pleasant that he wanted to continue it. For years he had not enjoyed his life of crime. Once begun, the game seemed to go on. There seemed to be no way out. Let them yell. Let them mock. Let them hate. He could not care.

Then a new voice sounded, closer to him than the crowd's. A weary voice, but shot through with a strange sweetness. Here was Someone, even on the hill of hate, who loved.

"Father, forgive them, for they know not what they do."

Dismas opened his eyes and slowly turned his head in the direction of the voice. Sharper pain twisted the taut muscles of his neck, but in that quick glance, he saw the face of Love. The eyes looked not at him, however, but down into the mob. Following that gaze, Dismas too looked down. There was a woman there in whose face he saw reflected the face of Love.

Who was she? Where did she come from? Why did the boy next to her not take her away from this gruesome place? Then he understood. Only a mother could look so at a son. She was the mother of the man crucified beside him. The man? Dismas understood more. No man spoke as this Man spoke, nor loved as this Man loved. Disregarding the pain, he turned again to the central cross.

"Lord, remember me when Thou shalt come into Thy Kingdom."

"Amen, amen I say to thee, this day thou shalt be with Me in Paradise."

AT CANA, John saw her first. Following Jesus closely into the crowded room, he caught a sudden vision of her loveliness as she stood, quiet, poised, half-smiling, among the serving women. She was unaware of their approach but turned quickly at the voice of Jesus.

They stood beside her then, and Jesus said, "Mother, this is John." No need to add, "my beloved friend." Hearts that love like hers have no need for such explanations. With all the graciousness of heaven's Queen, she turned to him, and John knelt swiftly, kissing the slender hand she held out to him.

⚘ 16 ⚘
QUEEN
AT
CANA

No one heeded this little scene in the noisy banquet hall where an impulsive boy bent over a beautiful woman's hand. And Jesus smiled. He saw John look at her as He had seen his young eyes raptured over a lake's white mystic beauty on a moonlit night. That soft intake of breath more eloquent than speech He too had heard from John when a pure white bird plunged out of a blue sky into a blue sea. Jesus was satisfied.

And John? She was not Mother to him now. That was for Calvary. She was his Queen, Queen of Beauty and of his youthful heart. Never again would the world's charm be anything else to him than a shadow of her radiance. This was his own miracle. The water of common earth was changed for him to the wine of heavenliness in her. Her wordless love made all creation sing a new song for him.

"You have kept the good wine until now," he heard the steward tell the bridegroom, and John nodded. Jesus alone was joy for all eternity, but now he had Jesus *and* Mary. This miracle also did Jesus at Cana of Galilee.

THE heart of Mary was always singing. From the un-beginning with God, she sang in His love. At creation she played and sang before Him, His daughter of delight.

He longed for her to exist in time, and the joy of Anne and Joachim at our Lady's conception and birth was nothing to the jubilee in the heaven of the Triune God.

Odd, quaint songs that children sing she sang for Him when she was small, but in the temple she learned His own music in the psalms. What wonder, then, when the joy of Jesus blossomed within her beauty after the Annunciation, that the happiness of mothering the Son of God should find expression in Hebrew psalmody? It was a true descendant of David who sang the *Magnificat*.

Elizabeth opened the door of the golden cage of song, and Mary's bird of happiness flooded the spring world with melody never heard before, even in heaven.

"My soul magnifies the Lord," she sang, her hands over her heart, her eyes on the pageantry of the hill country, green with budding life and sweet with April. "And my spirit rejoices in God, my Jesus."

St. Bernard would write centuries later: "The name of Jesus is honey to the lips." It was honey indeed on the lips of Mary and in the heart of Mary. The song Elizabeth heard — and the little unborn but bap-tized Baptist — would be more and more of joy to the world for whom His heart reached out in love in the first *Evangel* of His Mother. He was the good news that she announced, the lyric and melody of her song. Her song was Jesus.

THE signal for the beginning of the Sabbath sounded in Nazareth. Seated in the last rays of the setting sun, Mary snipped the final thread in her weaving and pulled a protecting cloth over her work. She rose slowly and went to the wide window on the street.

The sun caught her white gown and attracted to her a flight of doves. They flew about her like a cloud of white flames. They settled on her shoulders, her hands, as she stretched out her arms to them. Children hurrying past called out to her and the smiling woman waved a greeting. In flight as swift as their coming, the doves flew off.

Only one small one cuddled in the crook of her arm. She gently smoothed his feathers with her finger, laughing softly at his deep content. For him, too, it was the day of rest, even as it was God's Sabbath, who had finished His creation and saw that it was very good.

Forgetting the little dove, but continuing to stroke him, Mary let her mind go back to that first day of peace. Oh, the beautiful and wonderful world as it came from the hand of God. Who but He could know how excellent it was? Amid the wonders of His world stood the crown of His creation, Adam and Eve, resplendent in the gifts of His generous love. He rested not from fatigue, for He knew no weariness. His rest was a complete satisfaction in the task completed. To see the work well done and to be content in that sight — this is the true Sabbath.

The bird on her arm stirred. She lifted him against her cheek. So had her Jesus, the little bird of her heart, stirred in her arms in sleep. So long ago. And not again. For He too had had His day of rest. She raised her eyes to the sunset sky. Let Him rest, for His task also was ended. And His work too was very good.

SHE is the wise virgin who kept her lamp of faith alight through the night of Christ's humanity until His divinity dawned upon an unbelieving world.

She is the seed that fell upon good ground of grace and yielded fruit of good works a hundredfold. She is the tiny mustard seed, hidden and unknown, that grew into luxurious shade of hope for all to share.

She is the father of the prodigal, whose love draws wandering children home. She is the good Samaritan, binding the sinner's wounds and resting him in the shelter of her heart.

She is the seeking shepherd, after her sheep untiringly to bear him back to the fold of the Heart of God. She is the housewife busy with broom to find for us the silver coin of love.

She is the fisherman gathering into his net of vast solicitude the cares of all the children of men.

She is the merchant, giving all for the pearl of grace, digging the field of prayer for the priceless treasure of union with God. She is the king who calls all to the feast of heaven's joy in prayer.

She is the master of the vineyard. From dawn till dusk she summons laborers there, and at the end she rewards each with the vision of God.

She is the merciful farmer who let the cockle of distrust grow, lest the wheat of good will be also uprooted.

She is the leaven of holiness hidden in the meal of the world till the whole be sanctified.

She is, of all Christ's parables, the most telling and the true.

THE foxes had holes and the birds of the air nests, but Jesus laid His weary head at nightfall on the cushion of His folded cloak and slept beneath the olive trees. Starshine and moonlight canopied Him, as the shadows of the old branches swayed about His sleeping form.

There was a time when a woman's face had bent over Him, a little boy safe in His cozy bed in the home at Nazareth. There was a night when only her love kept Him warm in a cave's damp cold in Bethlehem. Hers was the tabernacle that had first housed His humanity after the Annunciation. She had been His home.

❧ 20 ❧
HOME
OF THE
HEART
OF GOD

Now, as He wandered, the Divine Vagabond, that shelter was still His. Over His sleeping head her faithful love kept vigil. Somewhere in the lonely night He knew that her heart watched. Never His eyes closed in weariness that He did not dream her sweet face above Him, and if He woke in the chill of dawn, it was to remember His mother's hands that wrapped Him tenderly in peace.

Over His sleep she spread a tent as of stars, each one a candle lighted for His joy. Night winds sang softly songs that only He and Mary knew. There was a benediction on His sleep that no one guessed, her smile that reached to Him, no matter how far the miles between them.

No cold, no rain, no fatigue too deep for slumber could rob Him of the comfort of her heart. This was His own, whatever the fortune of the road. Forever wandering, He found forever home.

Wanderers of night, may we not share her harboring? Mother of Jesus homeless, grant us His home in thee.

MARY knelt alone in her quiet room. It was early morning. Before the bustle of the day, this time was hers — for God.

What did she pray as she knelt unmoving? Or did she say a word, even in her heart? There is a love that needs no expression, and a desire that flames forth without a single breath. Did Mary simply long for God to come?

She had heard His voice thunder in the Scriptures, had seen the lightning of His words; but for His love, she knew there was no adequate symbol. He Himself must come to teach men that.

≥ 21 ≤

DAUGHTER

OF

DESIRE

"O God, my God, to Thee do I cry at break of day," she may have prayed in the words of the sacred singer. "For Thee my soul thirsts. . . ."

God thirsts to be thirsted for, St. Catherine of Siena wrote. And never a soul thirsted as Mary's for His advent. Hers was an irresistible desire. God came.

Thunders were stilled. Lightnings ceased. Out of the clear, bright dawn Gabriel spoke: "Hail, full of grace, the Lord is with thee." As if to say: "In love you have sighed for God. He is with you even now."

But Mary longed for another coming, one not for herself alone but for all the thirsting world. Would He not come for all God-longing men?

Gabriel continued: "The Holy Ghost shall come upon thee, the Power of the Most High shall overshadow thee, and He that shall be born of thee shall be called the Son of God."

This was the answer to her prayer of desire: *Emmanuel*, God with us, God within her for us.

ALL blessings fill the earth in Mary's prayer. Her life is our *Benedicite*. "Bless the Lord" is her continual cry.

Queen of Angels, she can command their glorious song.

Empress of the World, she can exact tribute of praise to God from crystal waters and high-flying clouds, from sturdy mountains and flowered fields. Sun, moon, and stars obey her behest to adore Him.

Lady of Light, she can bid night extol His glory as well as day. Not only suns obey her, but winds and storm; not only brightness and clear blue skies but darkness of deep midnight.

Mistress of Earth, trees lift hands to God for her, flowers bend in worship before their Lord at her command. Birds sing hosanna, and from furred creatures she may demand devotion for God, her Lord.

As Mother of Men, she can hymn praise with them: "Bless God, the Father, the Creator. Bless God, the Son, the Redeemer. Bless God, the Holy Spirit, the Sanctifier."

Blessed now, more than before, since her voice can call us to His love. Because of her, we dare to raise confident voice. Because of her, He will hear and be glad. Now, with her, we may sing more eloquently than Ananias, Azarias, Misael, than all the psalmists and singers of the ages before He came through her.

It is her voice for which He listens now — the sole unsinning one — who prays with Christ: "Blessed, O thrice-blessed be God now. Blessed be God forevermore."

Because He joys to hear her, He joys too to hear us. To praise God with Mary is to be heard with delight.

THROUGH all the psalms there is a note of victory. It is not a victory in hand of which the psalmist sings. It is an ultimate, assured triumph over his enemies through the strength of God.

The heart of Mary was in tune with this spirit of conquest. Long before the Resurrection, which was the victory above all victories for her Jesus, she celebrated the might of God. With the vision of the prophets, she foresaw eventual peace.

Therefore she sang "to the Lord a new song, for He has done wondrous deeds; His right hand has won victory for Him."

Sharing thus the sight of God, she glorified Him, and more than that, she rejoiced to sing the ancient paeans of triumph. God's victory roused her soul to more than strident conqueror's applause. It flooded her whole being with an undying gladness that welled up into jubilant song. Day after day she prayed with joy: "The Lord is King; let the earth rejoice, let the many isles be glad. . . . Light dawns, and gladness. Give thanks to His holy name."

Because she lived so close to Him, His triumph was a personal one for her, too. But she was more noble than to confine herself to selfish congratulations. Even as she had prayed for His coming to save all, she thanked Him and praised Him for saving all. This was her faith. Years and centuries must pass before the final battle for souls, but she knew in whom she believed.

And so she cried to all, asking them to join her in her prayer: "Sing joyfully to the Lord, all ye lands; break into song, sing praise, the world and those who dwell in it."

23

BEAUTIFUL in the morning sun lay the city of Jerusalem. Up to it came the pilgrims of God. Long lines of men and women lifted their eyes to the mount of God, lifted hearts to the God who dwelt there according to His promise. This was, to them, Paradise, the Garden of Eden where they might find and walk with the Creator.

Whatever their personal poverty, this richness was theirs. And they rejoiced because it was said to them, "We will go into the house of the Lord." To set foot within the gates of Jerusalem, to go up there with the tribes — this was their birthright and their great joy.

Strong towers and stately portals, wide courts and elaborate staircases, invaluable tapestries and golden hangings made up the shrine that was the center of the city. And in the midst of all, the sanctuary of God. Not strange that they loved it and prayed for peace within its walls.

Mary is more than the glory of Jerusalem. She is the holy city itself, beautiful and strong, the ark of the covenant and the shrine of God.

To her the tribes of the earth come up, giving thanks to the name of the Lord. In her virtues they find wealth that can never be strictly their own, but because it is hers, they can glory in it as a personal possession. In her peace they find peace. In her innocence they find purity. She is to them all that the old Hebrew city was to the people of God — a refuge and a stronghold and a palace of prayer.

A stream of hope gladdens the city of God. Hope in the heart of man, hope in the heart of Mary. "He who finds me finds life, and shall have salvation."

CLOSE to us as she seems in love, in care, in the dailiness of life, yet the thoughts of Mary rise to the highest heights. Her foundation stones are set in the holy mountain. Where others' holiness ends, hers only begins, and its peak is far, far out of our sight.

Above the humdrum of Nazareth's outward appearance, Mary reached to another world and walked in beauty with the All-Beautiful. Hers was an atmosphere too rarified for sin, a crystalline light which the children of Fatima to whom she appeared found themselves helpless to describe.

Watch the whitest cloud above the loftiest mountain. It is the hem of the garment of our Lady's sanctity. See the snow that fringes the pinnacle. Mary's blessedness begins there. It is known in full to God alone.

Should this abash us, or make us afraid of her who is Immaculate? This is God's own most holy mountain. Dare we try to climb it, even in thought? There is awe in the mere hint of this approach to infinity.

Mary has answered the question in her own life. She was not aloof. Common things were familiar to her. Her delights were to be with the children of men. There is no single incident that can be pointed out to show that she wants us to be strangers to her. In every apparition she has made herself supremely accessible to the lowliest. She has, in fact, made a point of appearing to the humble and poor. True greatness can afford to be humbled, and perfect sanctity is not afraid of sinful earth.

If she comes to us, condescending, it is to lift us to her heights, so that some day we may walk with her on the holy mountain of God.

25

OUR LADY
OF THE
HOLY
MOUNTAIN

ALL the hill country was waiting that quiet evening. Expecting she knew not what, Elizabeth sat beneath the vine that flowered at the door of the little stone cottage that was hers and Zachary's. An unreasoned gladness had filled the day, and tonight she listened to the silence intently.

Beyond the hedge rose the sound of footsteps. Someone was coming, and swiftly. Hand on her heart, she left her chair. Then she heard it, the sweet voice that belonged to only one person in the world, her cousin Mary. It called her name. How long now since she had seen the child in the temple, and yet there was no mistaking the lyric "Elizabeth" that rang through the evening air. Twice it was repeated, and then she saw Mary, running toward the house and into her arms.

≥ 26 ≤

OUR LADY

OF

GREETING

"Elizabeth!" she cried again, embracing her with love.

The hill country reverberated with the joy of that greeting. And Elizabeth learned the secret of such jubilee.

"Blessed art thou among women, and blessed is the fruit of thy womb. And whence is this to me, that the mother of my Lord should come to me? For behold as soon as the voice of thy salutation sounded in my ears, the infant in my womb leaped for joy. And blessed art thou that hast believed, because those things shall be accomplished that were spoken to thee by the Lord."

And Mary said, "My soul doth magnify the Lord: and my spirit hath rejoiced in God my Saviour."

Silence descended again upon the hill country. It had been the scene of the drama for which God had made it. To it Mary had brought "the desire of the everlasting hills."

THE Canticle of Canticles never ceases to amaze, with its lyric loveliness, daring figures of speech, unlimited richness of meaning. In it, God the Poet speaks. In it, God the Lover.

If this song of love is for all souls, above all it is for the most beautiful of all — Mary. Behind the wall of our human nature God stands, looking through the windows of her words, through the lattices of her thoughts. He speaks to her: "Arise and come."

"Make haste, my love, my dove, my beautiful one, and come."

Mary's desire for God hastened the Incarnation. Did God long for that union with her which it involved with equal ardor? The winter of waiting is over, the time of teaching men how impossible redemption without a Divine Redeemer. The rain of the tears of the prophets and holy ones from Adam down is over and gone. The flower of Mary has appeared, fragrant, fruitful. Her voice sounds in the dove calls, doves hidden in the clefts of the rock of her faith, in the hollow places of her humility.

Her voice is sweet. It sounds only the glory of God, His majesty, His greatness, His mercy. It sounds in His ear as a perfume of praise.

Her face is comely. She has shown it to Him always, but now it is raised in such an ecstasy of joy that He must say again that she is His beautiful one, His love.

Because He calls her by His will, she comes swiftly, like a roe or a young hart. She is His love, and all she has is His.

She is the Beloved of God.

THERE were long hours with Elizabeth after the singing of the *Magnificat* which Mary must have cherished. Such a summer would never come again, nor such companionship. Joy shared is doubled. And with no one would Mary sooner have shared her joy than with this holy kinswoman and friend, Elizabeth.

That there was more than joy is true. Joseph did not yet know of the Incarnation. Would God let him know as He had illumined Elizabeth? Mary could not tell. Only her faith trusted that all would be well.

As on all waiting, there was unfulfillment. Perfect joy was not yet.

So they sat often together in silent prayer, adoring, loving, and beseeching grace for all. The Lord was with them, truly. Here Mary can be most aptly styled Mother of Beautiful Love, of Fear, of Knowledge, and of Holy Hope.

To wait with her — what would it mean? What did Elizabeth learn in those sweet summer hours with the Mother of God?

PATIENCE to see suns rise and set, and no certitude for tomorrow.

EAGERNESS to do the will of God each succeeding minute, not asking to know what it might demand in the future.

GLADNESS in His Presence, confidence in His Love.

TENDERNESS toward all who must wait, perhaps fearfully, perhaps fretfully.

PRAYERFULNESS that makes the most idle-seeming time precious in grace.

Mary and Elizabeth — two women sewing in the soft sunshine — patterns for all who wait, for all who fear, for all who pray.

ALL the wise men of the world will bring her gifts. From the Magi's treasure down to the least child's handful of flowers laid at the feet of her statue, Mary is showered continually with tokens of love.

Artists sacrifice lives seeking the secret of depicting her beauty. Cathedrals from multiple hands swing aloft to praise her name. Tender and wistful melodies written to please her are sung by her children over the wide earth. Men bring incalculable wealth in many forms to set before her, the Queen of the Universe, the Empress of the World.

More than material riches will be brought, more than great talents. Led by the Son of God Himself, men will enslave themselves to her in love. To her they will give even their spiritual inheritance, their merits, their graces.

29
BRINGER
OF JOY

And she bends graciously to receive it all.

For in taking the tributes she knows that they are dust and ashes in comparison to the Gift that she has brought to us. Alone of all the world's women, she is the bearer of Life. Alone of all the world's philanthropists, she is the bringer of Joy.

Elizabeth knew it first, that this girl with the beautiful soul and voice was the Mother of God. Bearing Him, she bore all of Life and Beauty and Love.

We hear her still, singing out her greeting, and we reply: "What you bring is more than all, O Mary. What we give is what we have. Come, as to Elizabeth, and bring us Joy. That Joy we will return to you, with joy forever."

THIS was retreat. No murmur of the tumultuous world reached into the heart of the hill country. Zachary was silent of necessity; Mary and Elizabeth by choice. Wrapped in the singularly beautiful Presence of God, the little cottage seemed in solemn retreat.

The echoes of Mary's song filled the tranquil air. The triumph of her prophecy lingered to charge the commonplace with heavenly meaning. Creation in this tiny Paradise rejoiced with her in God, her Jesus.

Over their small daily tasks the two women sometimes spoke softly. Even these few words were of God and for God. Together they chanted the psalms, fresh now with a thousand interpretations they had never before suggested. A member of a priestly family, Elizabeth was far from ignorant of the depths and splendor of the Hebrew liturgy. She who had been prompted by the Holy Spirit to perceive Mary's secret honor was not slow to catch the undertones of meaning in the Messianic prayers.

Joy that was songful ecstasy sank to the more steady beat of thanksgiving and praise. Into the fabric of joy was woven the clear color of gratitude, the subtle humility of tremendous pride in God.

"He that is mighty hath done great things in me, and holy is His name."

This turning from self to God is the first lesson of Mary, the keynote of her spiritual life. Elizabeth learned it from her. John the Baptist learned it too. It was here that the outlook on life so characteristic of the saint of the desert was born. He learned the supreme lesson of detachment and attachment from Mary. He must decrease, surely, but only that God might increase and become his whole life as He was hers.

VII   OUR LADY OF SACRAMENTALS

Not strange that a mother should clothe her children.
Nor that the heavenly Mother should weave for her
earth children a luminous garb of grace, the wedding
garment without which all is darkness.

Yet wonder lies in this — that she should stoop to
throw about us a dull brown cloak of human weaving,
humble stuff fit for shepherds' coats and pilgrim hoods.

"Whoever dies clothed thus, shall enter heaven."

A blessed promise, if incomprehensible.

So they come from the ends of the world, wearing
the scapular of Mary. There are others more colorful,
flowers from the dark soil of Carmel, but this is the
earth that roots them. Lowly is the brown dirt, rich,
mellow, near-ocher, trampled and yet triumphant in
harvests lifted up to the blue heavens.

31

MADONNA OF THE CLOAK

This is the sign of her love, chosen by her own hand.
Not a cloak of many colors, for her sanctity is simple.
"The handmaid of the Lord," she called herself, and it
was humility that spoke. In the same quiet virtue she
garbs her children, those who have for elder Brother
Him who was meek and humble of heart. Those who
look for princely golden garments must be content to
wear on their pilgrimage a shepherd's rough apparel.

Only in heaven will the mystery of simplicity be
revealed. There the Queen, clothed in variety, shall
welcome her scapular-clad children. And as they look
on her they love, the beauty of Carmel will shine out,
and the dull cloth of their humility will take on an
eternal splendor. The cloak of Mary shall become the
glorious garb of God.

THIRTY pieces of silver clanged upon the stone floor of the temple before the contempt of the high priest's gaze, and Judas rushed out into perpetual night.

There was not one to gather up this silver for new minting. Must it be lost forever to the kingdom of God?

She who is humble will lift it up. She who is loving will mint it anew. She who is all-powerful with God's own strength will make it into currency for the children of His kingdom.

"Smooth and glowing with innocence again, my Mary, what impress shall it have?

COINER OF THE REALM

"Give it thy face, thy form, cast in an attitude of gracious giving, thy hands outstretched with love. Underneath thy feet the globe that is our world. Upon thy head the star-crown of thy queenship, and round about the words that sign the coin thine own and ours: O Mary conceived without sin, pray for us who have recourse to thee!

"Reverse it for the final imprint of thy hand. Place there the source of all grace, the cross of Jesus, and with it the letter $M - M$ for thy Mercy, M for thy Motherhood, M for the sweet name of Mary.

"And is that all? No, one more grace. For us the stars, emblems not so much of what you are to us, but of what we hope to be to thee: thy glory, thy delight. A Mother's crown is the sanctity of her children.

"With this silver coin, we purchase paradise!

"Men shall call this token thy miraculous medal."

THE gift was a rosary. But to the little girl who received it, beads were an ornament. Glittering chain, rose-colored beads, and at the end a dangling golden loveliness — what else to do but put it around her neck?

Older hands than hers have played with Mary's beads. Their toy. Their magic charm. Sinners will part from grace but not with this. Years may rust the gear of holiness but they will cling to a string of colored glass not held, perhaps, for decades, but safely tucked away in some private nook.

What the clue to this strange conduct? Having let real wealth go, why must they cherish what seems to be an empty bauble?

Because it is the concrete memory of their mother's hand. It is the single jewel remaining from their land of dreams. It is the slender thread of grace some day to lead them from the maze of selfishness to that Immaculate Heart where life begins.

The little hands will learn to say the beads once hung as jewelry. Before the might of the mystery of the words comes home to the child, she will say many Hail Marys. Over and over, bright bead by bead, she will call her "full of grace"; she will call her "Mother of God." Into the groove of slow routine will slip a thousand thoughts of her, a library of pictures linked with the sound of her name echoed endlessly.

This is the secret of Mary's rosary. So imperceptible its power that some scorn its strength. Only God will know, and the Mother of God, what miracles are wrought through this string of beads. It is this, held in the hand of Mary, that binds us to the Heart of God.

ALL the hot, dry summer cries for rain in the plaintive call of a dusty bird. Heat lies palpable, a haze over the hills. The metallic sun is cruel.

If, on the far horizon, that hand of cloud should again appear —

If, in the distance, a rumble of welcome thunder —

If, rushing over the torrid disk of sun, dark horsemen race —

With what ecstatic silence creation would await the promised rain! What precious havoc in the lashing wind! How rejoicing the smash of waves of silver water that smite the deep-dried earth as the Atlantic surf its long-suffering sands!

Holy water, we might call it. Not yet the fountain of living water that is grace, but a help to life, cleansing, cooling, revivifying.

So from our Lady's hands, as from the cloud of Elias, a swift downpour upon the dry soil of our indifferent hearts. So to awaken seeds of virtue in our souls, sudden showers of good intent from her pure inspiration.

Let the rains come, Lady of Life. Let fall the saving flood upon the poor parched lands. Men weep for rain. Men pray for rain. Men look with reddened lids through the terrible heat for the relief that you can bring to them. Only a word from you — and the world is drenched and delivered.

Send thy small cloud, Mary of Rains, and let the bird sing a rapture of praise for his plaintive pining. Free us from drought, Mother. Send us rain.

≫ 34 ≪
FRESHNESS
OF
SUMMER
RAIN

"I WILL light a candle for you at our Lady's altar," my dear child writes. I can see the picture clearly.

A slip of a girl in an early morning church before a votive shrine. Silver and blue the candles burning there. And she makes one more slight flame praise that silent Virgin, one more small life to burn out in praise to her.

Mary must love such candles. They carry her memory to tall, golden candelabra in the temple during her sheltered childhood. They take her even to rough red torches burning in shepherds' hands in the cave of Bethlehem. But more than all, they cloister her again at Nazareth, where a tender lantern-light revealed to her and Joseph the face of God.

"I will light a candle at our Lady's altar for you, too, little one," I shall write in turn to this dear child.

She knows that there will be no actual wax and wick, no flaming taper. Only in my heart will I light a thought of love in Mary, a joyous prayer of silver gladness and blue remembering.

Mary loves these candles more than vigil lights, for they renew the lamps of love lighted for her Jesus after Nazareth. Sweet oil of hospitality that burned for Him at Bethany. Garlanded, gay candles for Cana's blessed feast. And white Paschal lamps about the supper table in the Cenacle, the first Mass candles, as she and Jesus knew.

Sacred candles all, burn forever before Mary. Be to her blessed joy. Be to us blessed peace.

JOSEPH said nothing. Joseph had never said much, and, when his heart was deeply moved, he had no words at all.

But Mary knew. Love is instinctive in reading silences. When he had first come to her in the temple, she had realized without any explanation what he sought. His quiet eyes were eloquent with love even while the steady coolness of the hands he reached to her calmed what fear she might have had for her vowed virginity.

Joseph was strong. She had watched him in the small carpenter shop heave up beams of wood two men might struggle with in vain. Even his face was strong, with clean-cut features, deep-set eyes beneath unruly crisp dark hair. In his tones rang granite sincerity and a truth men could not doubt.

Mary sighed. On the still air she could hear his hammer now, a voice that said the things his lips would not. No steady calmness as before the angel came to her, but a quick staccato beat, perplexed, irritated, almost unkind.

What if she went soft-stepping over shavings and chips to lay her hand upon his arm and say, "Joseph, fear not. This is of God." All the vague shadows in his troubled eyes would vanish, and he would kneel with her in adoration.

But she must not. God's secret was His own. And He would send an angel to this man, so pure of heart, if He so willed.

Joseph was silent.

Mary was silent too.

God kept His secret.

⊱ 36 ⊰
OUR LADY
OF
ST. JOSEPH

HERS is the silent flame from which the runners light their torches. Then into the rushing wind their feet speed to the ends of the world to announce her Christ.

Only one man kneels constant before her an hour, studying the varied grace in that bright flame of love, the face of the Mother of God. Luke knew that there was color and beauty here that he would never find again.

Out of the sacred night in which her flame burned in the hidden hall, Luke bore a portrait, done not in pigment but in the magic of words. From the sweet, silent woman he had won fragments of brightness that he placed in patient skill upon the new gold of his Gospel. Mosaic more brilliant than Giotti's frescoes — more full of light.

Runners and torches go on through the centuries. Hand thrusts into hand the undying faith that sprang from the Holy Spirit that first Pentecost. But Luke's lightsome pictures hold a deeper warmth than the acts of the martyrs, than confessors' deeds of acclaim. Theirs is the wonder of grace, but his is the mirror of her, the heart of grace. Theirs is the primitive strength of men; his is the delicate wonder of the Woman of Women, the Bride of God.

Hidden in his Gospel is the flame of the Cenacle, the sanctuary light first lighted there by the Spirit of God. Light of the Spirit is the light of love. And Mary's heart held first that tiny spark of Love that was to be the God-Man, that was to be the Eucharist.

He has captured in words the joy of God's Heart, the face of beauty forever smiling.

"No ROOM in the inn," they said. No room for God.

And we reply: "Call down fire from heaven, O powerful Mother. Open again, Omnipotent Suppliant, the floodgates of Divine Wrath. Defend the right of the God indwelling thee, who seeks a place to rest among His own."

But Mary, with no word, no gesture, turns with patient Joseph from the unfriendly town.

This is her reply: "They call upon themselves the fire of desolation to whom God comes beseeching and who will not heed Him. Forever and forever they will want for Him whom they rejected. To the far ends of the wide earth they will seek Him. The flames of unfulfilled desire will be their hell.

"Into the flood of thirst they cast themselves from whom He asks the water of hospitality, and asks in vain. Here unrecognized is the fountain for quenching all their longing. Refusing it, they wander in the desert of frustration for the endless years.

"Better the cold of the cave than their torturing fire. Better the damp of a winter night in the open than their barren death. Theirs to be pitied; mine to be pitiful."

Silent the cave on the hillside, and warm with love. Noise chokes the town behind them, frozen in discontent.

Theirs was the great mistake: not to know the time of God's visitation.

Theirs the eternal penalty: to wait for Love who have selfishly sent Love from their door.

Our Lady was beyond ecstasy. Conceived immaculate, she had prayed a perfect prayer before her birth. The child who grew in the home of Joachim and Anne knew how to pray. And when, in the temple, she was taught the psalms and ceremonies so dear to Jewish hearts, the words and actions only channeled deep waters of pure prayer already in her soul.

To pray in words was not beneath her, but it was no more than an expression of the constant prayer in her heart, the breath of her life. The Lord who was always with her needed no words for Mary's love. He understood her silent uplifted look of prayer.

Quiet the stream in the quiet wood. Silent the bird swinging high above the earth. So was Mary's prayer.

With joy she would sing *Magnificat*, her praise of God, the echo of the lyric love in her heart always. But on Calvary there is no gospel word quoted as from her lips. The garden of the Resurrection is conspicuously silent.

It was in the Cenacle that Mary's prayer is spoken about in a telling phrase: the Apostles were "persevering in prayer with Mary, the Mother of Jesus," writes St. Luke. It was as if she taught them her secret of silent adoration and thanksgiving and reparation and petition. In that first retreat, she gave them lessons in mental prayer and the loving thought of the things of God with God that leads to the heights of contemplation. Yet all without a single syllable.

Mary taught prayer by the exquisite beauty of her own inner life. Mary taught prayer with silent love.

SHE is the Queen of those who never find the final bullet, whose martyrdom is not a single sweep of the beheading sword. She is the Mother of those who walk the long road to Calvary, doggedly, in silence, alone.

St. Thomas More, with his head on the block, might jest. Miguel Pro could cry exultantly, *"Viva Christo Rey:* Long Live Christ the King," and then fall before Mexican bullets. But it was not in that last high moment that heroism lay, nor sanctity. In a life of fidelity to commonplace duty, Thomas More was lawyer, chancellor, husband, father, friend. It was the long road that led to the longer wait in the Tower of London that prompted that light word at the end of the patient silence of St. Thomas More.

For Miguel Pro, Jesuit priest and martyr of the twentieth century, the odyssey of life from Mexico to Texas to Spain to Lourdes to Central America and back to Mexico was antecedent and preparation for the moment in the prison yard. The strength of the hidden years welled up in that crisis, the stored grace of the silent sacrifices of youth and early manhood. It was his silence that cried out to Christ, his King.

There was a child who seemed to win, in one short space of time, the crown of martyrdom — St. Maria Goretti. But it was not so. All that little one's life of devotion to her parents, to her smaller brothers and sisters, all the vigils of sleepless nights of terror and the silence of days of imminent peril formed the price of that heroic stand against sin and that heroic forgiveness that evokes the admiration of a noisily impure world. She walked with Mary the long road to life.

POLICE cars roar through the city streets. Banners are hung high over all. Crowds mill along the sidewalks of the line of march. In the distance there is music, a haunting melody sung by many voices. Alternately with it is the steady beat of rhythmic prayer.

This is not a parade but a procession. Shoulder to shoulder they come along, school children, sodality girls, rosary society women, squires and knights, Holy Name men, the Legion of Mary, nuns, brothers, priests. And at the end? A small, white wooden statue of our Lady of Fatima, sweet faced and wistful, her golden crown graceful, her pearl rosary hanging from delicate fingers.

In former times, men went on pilgrimage to Mary. Today she comes to them.

For they have forgotten her, if ever they knew her. They do not recognize this Mother. Bethlehem and Nazareth are only myths to them, and Calvary a place of historic note.

Traveling from place to place, imitating the journeys of Jesus, Mary seeks her children. And when she comes, she teaches them to pray. Many admonitions she gave to the children at Fatima, but above all, to pray the Rosary. As she said it with Bernadette, so now she says it with her more destitute children of the Atomic Age, teaching them, through its words and mysteries, the love of Christ.

For at the end of each procession, Mary steps aside. The statue is placed near an altar, and Mass is said, or Benediction given. The custom is unfailing. Mary has turned pilgrim only to bring the world to the feet of Christ, the Son of God.

§ 41 §

THE
PILGRIM
VIRGIN

At the Bishop's command, the Indian Juan Diego opened his cloak. In it he guarded a miracle, as he knew. For when the Lady had said, "Go, gather roses on the mountain as a sign," he had gone to the December peak and found red roses in the snow, more beautiful than dawn and more fragrant than the scent of tropic gardens.

Now he let fall the ends of his rough shepherd's wrap, and from its fold cascaded brilliant flowers. The hostile face of the Bishop changed completely. Sardonic eyes lost their hardness in a glance of wonder. He knelt down.

Juan stepped back in dismay. Roses — even Mary's miracle roses — would not win this homage. Then he too saw. Upon the cloak he still held in his hands was a picture. The Lady! His Lady. And he knelt also, clasping to his heart the picture of his Queen.

Over the Mexican mountain peasants came. And kings. Through the long years our Lady of Guadalupe gathers roses for the children who kneel at her shrine. In dark ages of persecution, her marvelous portrait remains unharmed. Not even modern bombs can shake the citadel of her love.

If with the roses she gives there remain small thorns of pain, her children do not complain. Only by clasping her roses of love and of faith, can they be certain to hold in their hearts the vision of her loveliness and the power of her pleading for them.

They hope, like Juan Diego, so to look one day upon her face. In their winter world, she is their Rose of Beauty. In heaven, she will be their Rose of Eternal Joy.

GAY children danced at Fatima. Round and round on the hillside small Jacinta's feet twinkled, her bright skirt swirled. Taller Lucia caught her hands and swung her about again. Francisco played faster on his little flute. Only the sheep grazed quietly in the strong Portuguese sunshine.

Then the light began to change. The dancing children stopped to talk with a beautiful Lady. They danced no more. Was the glory of their Lady's love enough of joy for them?

"O children, dance for us again!"

"No, no, we do not want to dance! Let the sun dance!"

Gathered in the October sky like a giant pinwheel, the sun began to dance. It twirled and twisted with a thousand rainbow lights. It reflected in the faces of the people and set the whole world afire with colored flame. It swung out of its orbit near the earth.

"O Lady, stop the dance! We are afraid!"

And the dance stopped. High in the heavens the sun climbed again. Placid and commonplace, it resumed its place.

The world waits. When will the sun dance once more? Is the joy of Mary's glory now confirmed? Or must it learn in terror what the children learned in love?

"Lady, Mistress of the Dance, teach us to love!"

Your children dance in the sun of your love. The sun dances in the children's delight. Joyous and carefree, the world may dance if it will.

"Lady, Mistress of Love, teach us to dance!"

Sᴉsᴛᴇʀ Mᴀʀɪᴇ Bᴇʀɴᴀʀᴅ, who had been Bernadette of Lourdes, was dying in her convent at Nevers, France. The doctor looked at the nurse and shrugged. What hope was there? A man could do no more.

"Unless," he said reflectively, "you want to take her to Lourdes."

The magic word roused the still figure on the bed. Bernadette's beautiful dark eyes opened.

"Lourdes," he repeated, smiling at her gently. "Why shouldn't your Lady cure you there with all the others?"

Bernadette smiled back at him, but shook her head weakly. He bent to hear what she said.

"The grotto is not for me," she whispered earnestly.

How long ago it seemed that she had sat down that February afternoon beside the shallow stream over which her companions had gone before her? Then a rustle of wind, a glance upward, and the whole world was changed forever in her eyes. In the rocky cavern had been a message for her to carry.

"Tell them this, tell them that," the Lady had said.

Faithfully, Bernadette had repeated it all.

Should she have remained at the grotto when the messages were over? Might there not have been a message for her?

Bernadette smiled to herself, but said no more. The doctor left without saying more of Lourdes. He did not know what Bernadette knew.

Alone in the room she murmured again, "The grotto is not for me. For me, my Lady is enough."

OTHER shrines have statues. Loreto has emptiness. It is shell within a shell within a shell. Marble and gold and beauty are there, but in the center, only a poor little house. And in the house, only one small room. And in the room only a plaque saying:

HERE THE WORD WAS MADE FLESH

To kneel on that spot where the Angel of the Lord declared unto Mary, pilgrims have journeyed miles and miles. More pilgrims have come to Loreto than to any other shrine in the Christian world. Its emptiness is magnetic.

For within the house now guarded by angel hands, Mary dwelt. She was the smaller house of God that made this one so precious. Body of Mary, soul of Mary — O House of God.

It is this emptiness that attracted the God of Hosts, the great God of Creation and Redemption and Sanctification, to enter into her smallness. Marble and gold He values less than nothing. What won Him was the purity of Mary, the invitation of her love for Him to come. For Him the peace of Mary, the quiet of her listening to His voice. For Him the emptiness of Mary, her whole self lifted up for Him to fill. Here, in fact, the Word was made flesh.

God winged the Holy House of Loreto with angels to take it into peace. God gave angels to Mary on the day of the Assumption to take home His more precious house, the body of His Mother. The shell of God in heaven is not emptiness. It is to this Holy House that Loreto pilgrims really turn. Because of her, the little house enshrined is holy. Kneeling there, they lift their hearts to her.

ST. FRANCIS loved a lady, the Lady Poverty. Because of her he walked barefooted, alone, in pain.

St. Francis loved the Mother of God, our Lady. Because of this, out of his poverty, he gave her gifts.

Rare jeweled slippers Francis gave our Lady, dainty kid shoes with flowered tongues and slender golden cords. For her, God would open wide roads of grace, and on her way, St. Francis and his sons would sing her slippered feet to dancing.

That she might not walk alone, St. Francis called to comrade her the heaven full of angels. Into one small house he crowded all of Paradise to make a melody for Mary, Mistress of Angels. No housewife is she in Francis' Portiuncula, but a Queen enthroned with her celestial court. Upon her knee, her Little One, the King of Angels, and round about, gay lyre and silver flute and all manner of minstrelsy.

St. Francis gave her memory of joy. For him Alvernia and a winged seraph bearing pain. But for her, remembrance clear of seven joys, a thousand joys, oh, endless joys! Let her forget all but the luminous words of Gabriel, of Elizabeth, of the *Gloria*. Let her remember a little face against her cheek and Joseph's smile. If she must recall the wounds of Jesus, let it be those glorious gems of Easter morning. Francis would give her only joy.

At the door of the House of the Angels kneels a barefooted friar in a coarse robe girded with a rope. To him will our Lady bring with her own hands, the Cause of Joy, the Child of God, her Jesus.

≥ 46 ≤

QUEEN

OF

ST. FRANCIS

MICHAEL the Archangel watched a child at play. This little girl, frail and delicate and dainty, was a pretty thing. He waited as the wind blew her soft dark hair about her smiling face with its small mouth and beautiful eyes.

Should Michael go now and pay homage to this Mary? Shining and tall, he stood as once he had stood upon the parapet of heaven and seen Lucifer fall to hell beneath his flaming sword.

But there had come another day. When Lucifer had returned, serpent-wise, to trick poor Mother Eve, Michael had heard a prophecy. Adam and Eve went forth from the garden, as bidden, and seraphim lifted fiery weapons to guard the gates against their future entrance there. Then God spoke. He said: "I will establish a feud between thy offspring and hers; she is to crush thy head, while thou dost lie in ambush at her heels."*

She shall crush thy head, Michael mused. Not Michael's sword this time. The battle was to the weak. Heaven's combat was over and strong Michael had won. But earth's battle had only begun.

A little girl playing at her mother's knee looked up as the sunlight vanished. She was not afraid when Michael stood before her. His brighter sunshine lighted up her loveliness as at her feet he laid his gleaming sword.

The leader of all the angels acknowledged Mary his Queen.

---

* Gen. 3:15. Translation of Ronald A. Knox (New York: Sheed and Ward, Inc., 1948). This verse of Genesis is none too clear in the Hebrew, and most Scripture scholars today believe that the words should read, "He [or It] shall crush thy head." That the reference of the passage is to the Incarnation is, at any rate, the general opinion of the Fathers. And Mary, as Mother of the Incarnate Word, is rightly considered as vanquisher of Satan.

So STILL the fields — as if a starry blanket had been laid upon the heavens. As if all the winds were drugged. The young shepherd caught his breath in sheer wonder at the beauty of the night. How could men sleep away hours like these? The sheep? Yes, just stupid animals. But men who could see it! Not even a dog stirred in the quiet. A fire kept barely burning crackled only now and then. A sleeping shepherd moaned.

Then it happened. As if stage curtains rolled back, the starry skies parted. Night brightened to more than morning. An angel stood before him as the other shepherds started up from their sleep.

☙ 48 ❧

THE YOUNG SHEPHERD'S *GLORIA*

"Fear not, for behold I bring you good tidings of great joy, that shall be to all the people. For this day is born to you a Saviour, who is Christ the Lord, in the city of David. . . ."

And suddenly there was with the angel a multitude of the heavenly army, praising God and saying: "Glory to God in the highest, and on earth, peace to men of good will."

The young shepherd was the first to rise to go. Let us hurry! Let us hurry! And they found Mary and Joseph, and the Infant.

The bright-eyed boy knelt at Mary's feet. Star-studded heavens were beautiful, but not like this. Angel songs were marvelous, but none like this. This woman's face was Beauty, and her glance at the God within her arms sang a *Gloria* not even angels knew.

WE PRAISE THEE, WE BLESS THEE, WE ADORE THEE, WE GLORIFY THEE, WE GIVE THEE THANKS. . . . O LAMB OF GOD, O LAMB OF GOD!

BEAD by bead, ravel out! The words — half said, whole said, careless said, fervent said; Latin, English, polyglot. Beads — crystal, wooden, twist of cord. Hands — youthful, hardened, wrinkled and old. Scene — grotto, sickbed, ambuscade.

Bell by bell, ravel out! *Angelus* tinkle at dawn in cloister towers; big bell booming in churches at the city's noon; gentle tones pealing through the countryside in evening cool.

Soul by soul, ravel out! Last saint smiling at grim death drawing on, beads in hand to baffle the grave; last sinner hoping against hope in Mary's merciful heart and name; whole world of men from Elizabeth to now.

Ravel out, ravel back, Angelus, Rosary, last cry to Mary, and what can you find but this scene? A little room in Nazareth, a praying girl, and an angel named Gabriel.

This the angel chosen by God for this drama of the Incarnation. It is his moment supreme. God's great ambassador comes to a maid. And it is the words he said to her that we ravel out, his voice the first of all bells to proclaim them.

"Hail, full of grace. The Lord is with thee. . . ."

Ravel out the threads of the prayer, of the bell. It is Gabriel's word. It is God's gift to him. It is Gabriel's gift to Mary and to us.

Ravel out the threads of the souls who have loved his words, who have loved the girl to whom he spoke them and have trusted in her name. It is their hope of heaven.

LED by the Spirit, Jesus spent forty days of fast in the desert, and afterward, He was hungry. Then the devil came to tempt Him until Jesus said, "Begone, Satan."

Weary the lonely Christ leaned against a rock. Somewhere in Galilee, His Mother prayed.

"And behold, angels came and ministered to Him."

Jesus prayed in the garden of Gethsemani. The dark olive trees brooded above Him. The Apostles slept near. He was alone in His great agony.

Somewhere, perhaps in Bethany, His Mother prayed.

"And there appeared to Him an angel from heaven, strengthening Him."

50

MISTRESS

OF

ANGELS

Mary Magdalen and the other women came to the sepulcher, the sun having risen. And they said to one another, "Who shall roll us back the stone from the door of the sepulcher?"

In the brilliant sunshine of that morning, a woman with a face full of joy prayed for those who had not yet seen the risen Sun.

And looking, the women saw the stone rolled back. For it was very great.

And entering into the sepulcher, they saw a young man, clothed with a white robe, who said to them: "You seek Jesus of Nazareth who was crucified. He is risen, He is not here. Behold the place where they laid Him."

Hail, O Queen of Heaven enthroned!
Hail, by angels mistress owned. . . .

INTO the great hall of Paris University walked Duns Scotus. Sharp faces watched him, his monk's robe swishing above sandaled feet, his features half-hidden in his brown hood.

He would try today, they whispered to each other, to prove the Immaculate Conception of the Mother of God. St. Thomas Aquinas had been against it, and St. Bernard. The people with their emotional nature and untrained minds were with him, yes. But what was their tradition against the logic of the schools?

Duns Scotus began to speak.

"Potuit," they heard him say. God *could* do it. To preserve His Mother immaculate was surely within His divine power. By a preventative grace, earned by the redemption of Christ, He could save her from the slightest stain of original sin.

"Decuit," he continued to explain. It was *fitting* that God do this. She who was to be the Mother of His Son should be free of any least momentary humiliation beneath the dominion of Satan. She should shine re-splendent with grace from the instant of her conception.

The vast lecture room was hushed to complete silence.

"Ergo," the intense voice rang out, and Scotus, drop-ping his hands in a gesture of conclusion, raised his head in quiet challenge. His hood slipped back to reveal a luminous face. *"Ergo, FECIT."* Therefore, God did it.

He let the echo of his voice die out in the electrified atmosphere. With no more to say, he walked with deliberate steps from the room.

51

LADY

OF

DUNS

SCOTUS

"WHAT is His name?" admiring people asked our Lady as she lifted the light blanket from her Baby's face so that they could see Him.

Her gentle voice would reply, "We call Him Jesus."

Into their eyes would come a look of awe. "Jesus — the Saviour." What might this child not become? But then they soon forgot.

Centuries of anguished waiting led behind that name, and centuries of grateful remembering. It is at once the most beloved name and the most hated. Mystics go into ecstasy to hear it. Vile men use it to vent their wrath.

"What is His name?" men asked on the first Good Friday, passing up the hill of skulls on their way to the holy city. Those around the cross pointed to its inscription: Jesus of Nazareth, the King of the Jews.

"A Jesus," jibed His enemies, "A strange Saviour this! Let Him come down from the cross and we will believe."

But Jesus was silent. This was salvation, that He die for them. This justified His name forever.

Men in later times, He knew, would recognize the power of that name, would bear it on banners and blazon it on shields. Imitating Mary's reverence, heads would bow to hear it, as angels knelt and demons raged.

When comes the end of the world, and the sign of the Son of Man appears in the heavens, this name shall shine upon it: Jesus, Saviour. Then the united voices of all men shall sing with Mary His praises. With her they will love that Holy Name.

"MARY is taken up into heaven. The angels rejoice. . . ."

How long they have waited for her to come, their Queen, even through the uncounted ages. Even where time was not, there can be aeons of longing.

And now she comes. Below Apostles weep for their Mother's death, and lagging Thomas says, "Where have you laid her?"

Where they have laid her does not matter now, Thomas. She is not there.

For in the sweet dawn light, hymns of angels wakened her from slumber. Rising to that call, she left her couch and lifted her eyes to heaven. It was not angels her eyes sought, nor them she saw. It was her Jesus. But swiftly they came, her angel bands, and with them carried her up to the God who waited for her, eager to pay homage to this Mother whose life had been all homage to Him.

It is His joy that all heaven echoes. It is His joy her own heart cherishes as she is received into the celestial courts as its Queen. If there is joy in heaven upon a sinner's doing penance, how much more a measure of jubilee for this triumphant homecoming of her who knew no sin?

"Mary is assumed into heaven. The angels rejoice, and with praises bless the Lord."

Below, Thomas rolls back the stone. All the loveliness of summer gardens blossoms within the tomb. She is not there. Behold the place where they laid her. Rejoice with the angels, for Mary has gone home.

WE PRAISE thee, O Mary; we acknowledge thee to be our Queen.

All the earth doth honor thee, the Mother of God and man.

To thee all the angels cry aloud, the heavens and all the heavenly powers.

To thee the cherubim and seraphim do cry: Thou art our Queen.

Heaven and earth unite in honoring thee.

The glorious choir of the Apostles praise thee.

The admirable company of the Prophets praise thee.

The white-robed army of Martyrs praise thee:

Daughter of the Father of infinite majesty,

Mother of the adorable, true, and only Son of God,

Also the Spouse of the Holy Spirit, the Comforter.

Thou art the Queen of Glory, O Mary!

Thou art the Mother of God.

When He took on Himself to deliver man, He did not disdain thy womb.

Thou sittest in heaven, His Queen forever.

We therefore pray thee to help thy children, whom He has redeemed with His precious blood.

Make them to be numbered with the saints in glory everlasting.

Govern them and raise them up forever.

Every day we bless thee, and we praise thy name, forever and ever.

Have mercy on us, O mother of Mercy, as we have hoped in thee.

In thee have we trusted. Let us not be confounded forever.

⊁ 54 ⊀

OUR LADY

OF THE

TE DEUM

MARY echoed the angel of the Ascension:

Stand not here looking up into heaven.

Not in the cloud — not in the vain remembrance of things past, however holy —

Not in the nebulous cloud of words vaguely recalled, however wise —

Not in the futile longing for what has been, and can never be again, however joyous —

Christianity is forward.

Turn from the white cloud to the grimy city. Men need to hear of Jesus Christ.

Turn from the city to the cenacle of peace. Prepare for your apostolate by prayer.

Turn from the city and the cenacle to the God present within you by grace. Be one with Him. Here is your strength.

Why stand you here? Christianity is forward.

To stand is not Christian, except to stand *for* or *against,* to take a stand for Christ.

To kneel first is good. Pray for guidance and grace. But then step boldly into the marketplace to trumpet Christ. Men who would not hear Him will hear you. Yours shall be the harvest of His pain. As He promised, greater works than His shall you do. Be confident.

Christianity is forward. You can do all things in Him who strengthens you.

Go forth and teach all men. . . .

GIFTS of the Magi glittered in Mary's hands. Her hands caressed the shapely jar of myrrh, the costly, delicately carved chest in which the fragrant incense lay. These were craftsmen's creations of beauty, and for that she loved them. But the jingling coins in their heavy bag did not win her caress. Quieting their noise clatter, she ranged them beside the other gifts without a word.

Joseph watched her face for some indication of her thought. He was a poor man but not destitute. He had married her in the hope that he might care for her, simply but adequately. There was a further question now. Would that simple care be enough for God's Son? Dared he refuse this wealth thrust so suddenly into their hands?

≫ 56 ≪

QUEEN

OF THE

POOR

As though she read his mind, Mary smiled at him. In that smile he read her deep content with their poverty, her trust in his strong hands to provide for her and Jesus.

"Tomorrow," she said, still smiling, "you'll make a small box, Joseph, and we shall keep the gifts for Him."

He nodded eagerly. That was it. When Jesus was of age, He might use the gifts as He pleased.

Neither Mary nor Joseph guessed that, in another night, they would be on their way, gifts and Child, to Egypt, and happy to use there the treasure of the Magi. So that the grown-up Child would hear His Mother tell the story, always to add, "God provided for us in that strange land." And Joseph would agree thoughtfully, saying, "Our God was good."

ONE by one, the words that Mary said settled to a single chord.

Her conversation with the Angel Gabriel at the Annunciation sounded the key note. Her question, "How can this be done. . . ?" indicated that perfect open heart that is necessary for the beginning of sanctity. She had a vow of virginity. What the Angel said did not seem to permit her to keep it. But she was willing to hear more of God's plans in the matter. When she learned that, she asked no further question. Without hesitation she said: "Behold the handmaid of the Lord. Be it done unto me according to thy word."

More lyrically she said the same thing, with additions that threw the sound of her perpetual harmony with God's will across the world. A clear high note of greeting to Elizabeth led to the full song, *Magnificat*. It was her song of thanksgiving that God had used His handmaid according to His most glorious plan, despite her unworthiness, loving her lowliness because she gave it simply to Him.

Then a low, sad note was addressed to Jesus. "Why hast Thou done so to us?" His reply was all she needed, however. Had He chosen to continue "about His Father's business," Mary would have made no remonstrance. His reward for her docility was His return to Nazareth for eighteen years.

Her last words harmonized perfectly with her first. Her concern for the Cana couple is similar to her query to the Angel. Her reply to Jesus is equally submissive, and, at the same time, a token for all who would follow her example: "Whatsoever He shall say to ye, do." It summed up her whole life and its complete harmony with the music of God's will.

Such a multitude of people who crowded to see Jesus that morning, John told our Lady enthusiastically — and He taught them to pray!

Mary's face was as eager as his own as she listened to the boy. Had she not seen Jesus pray?

The clear voice rushed on with the story.

"And Jesus said, 'When ye pray, be not as heathens, but say: Our Father who art in heaven, hallowed be Thy name; Thy kingdom come; Thy will be done on earth as it is in heaven . . .'"

More than that Mary did not hear. Immersed in the excitement of repeating the beautiful words — oh, never, never had man spoken as this Man! — John did not notice that she had ceased to listen to him.

One phrase only rang in her ears: Thy will be done on earth as it is in heaven.

For Mary, that was the supreme prayer. The heart of all prayer. The prayer perfect. She had said it in her own words from the beginning. She had said it in her whole life.

But how wonderfully satisfactory to have the formula of Jesus in which to say it. Should not God's Son know best how to speak to His Father? This was the way it would be said by the world that loved Him until the end of time, until that part of which it spoke was dissolved in eternity, and there was praising God heaven alone.

Conscious at last that Mary was not listening, John paused. She answered his silence with a quiet word. "Say it again, John, slowly. And let me say it with you."

"Our Father who art in heaven . . . Thy will be done . . ."

LONG trains, crowded buses, autos and ambulances roll out of Lourdes, their freight of human misery about equal in exit to that at entrance. Yet, in the departing sick, there is no sign of discontent, of anger at an unpropitious goddess.

This is the miracle of Lourdes. Not the many that are cured of physical ills but the many not embittered by the refusal of their Lady to cure them. After her denial, their love and faith remain the same.

It is as if, at Lourdes, there are children of Cana and children of Calvary. To her children of Cana, Mary says: "For joy our Jesus changes the water of your weakness to the wine of strength."

But to her children of Calvary she says nothing. In the dark night of suffering she goes with them to kneel, like Jesus, in the Garden of Gethsemani. Together with them she repeats His prayer: "Father, if it be possible, let this chalice pass from Me. Yet, nevertheless, not My will but Thine be done."

It is more than a prayer of faith. It is an invitation to Calvary. The alternative to the passing of the chalice is always the same. Those who pray thus with Jesus in the Garden will inevitably pray with Him on the cross in filial abandonment: "Father, into Thy hands I commend My spirit."

This is the miracle of Lourdes, and its greatest lesson. From the smiles of those who leave uncured and still singing *"Ave, Ave, Ave Maria"* men learn again that "in His will is our peace."

HER perfect love would not say no to Him, her Jesus. If He wanted her to remain on earth till the end of the world, Mary would say: "Be it done unto me according to Thy word."

Yet there was not a sacrifice greater to be asked of her now. All her life, back to its immaculate beginning, had been His, and in Him. That could not change now. But she had known the exquisite peace of His Presence — the sound of His voice, the touch of His hands, even His wounded hands, the light of His eyes. She had known all the litany of gospel places with Him: Nazareth, Bethlehem, Jerusalem, Egypt, Cana, Capharnaum, Bethany, the Cenacle, Calvary. . . . She had seen Him weak and needing her. She had seen Him strong in a strength far beyond her. She had held Him dead in her arms and then looked upon His risen loveliness. She had seen Him, after all that, ascend into heaven, leaving her upon earth.

It could never be the same again, not even with the Mass, not even with Holy Communion. No matter how holy her resignation to His will, her mother's heart would long for Him, and every step would be a step in exile from Jesus who was her heaven.

Death can come from love. Death can come from longing. And Mary's life, as the years went by, was consumed in both. The infant Church grew under her watchful eye. One by one the Apostles went on their missions to teach all men until only John remained with her. God's will only mattered to her, but oh, the joy when that will called her home. It was with smiling lips she said to that summons, as to all the others, "Thy will be done."

HE WAS not far. He had never been far from her. After the Ascension there was, between Jesus and Mary, only the door of heaven.

And yet it was a separating door. She could not see His face or hear His voice. No longer at dawn on the sweet winds of morning would come His loving call. Only a silent Host in the hands of John told her that Jesus was near.

In the silence her faith found Him, but her heart longed for the fullness of His Presence. Her life was an expectation. She lived in time while her heart waited for eternity. When would she go, according to His will, home to His heart?

Those who have yearned for the sight of a beloved face, a familiar landscape, a cherished dwelling place know with what joy Mary ended her exile.

Carefully she gathered up the fragments of the days apart from Jesus and laid them aside. Before her stretched the wholeness of eternal gladness in perfect union with God.

Quiet as the garden of the Resurrection had been, this garden of the Assumption was more still. Not an angel came to say, "She has been taken away to heaven." Only the lilies grew, silent and white. Only the sun shone, serene and uncommunicative.

Somewhere was jubilee. Somewhere an exultation thrilled all Paradise as Mary came home to Jesus. Somewhere a Queen was greeted by her king amid an admiring court. Somewhere a Mother held her Child again to her heart. Somewhere Mary found her Jesus.

61

OUR LADY
OF
HOME-
COMING

HAPPY the house of Lazarus at Bethany when Jesus visited it. Martha was astir before daybreak to begin the preparations for a royal welcome for the Master. With her arose Mary, and together they spent the day making ready for His coming at eventide.

When He had come, Mary knew one courtesy alone — to sit at His feet and listen to His words. Food for His body was ready, and rest for His weariness. The duties of hospitality had been taken care of.

But He had another need. Love lives in giving more than in taking. It was the joy of His heart to give. Food for the spirit lay in His eloquence, and rest for her soul. Should she not let Him give to her? She had only to listen to be satisfied. The craving of her soul for life and truth was satisfied in the words of the Word.

Mary was Mary. Mary will always be Mary. From Mary, the Queen of All Saints, to Mary, the last sinner forgiven because she has loved much, there will always be Marys to catch this innermost desire of the heart of Christ. They will sit at His feet and listen — a gesture of courtesy more indicative of love than endless service. The one thing necessary is love. For them, this is love's service.

Let Martha be busy about many things. It is her way of serving God. But let Mary sit with Jesus, silent, attentive, tranquil. This is her grace, to listen to the voice of the Beloved and, hearing, to fill the deep longing of His generous heart.

For all eternity she can do no more. This is heaven begun. Mary has chosen this better part, which will not be taken away from her forever.

Now is the mirror of justice ashine over all the world, its sun of peace. Now has our Lady entered into her own.

Now is the throne of wisdom enshrined in the house of God, resplendent in the palace of the Trinity.

Now is the costly spiritual vessel carried by angel hands, a vessel of honor, a vessel of such singular devotion that no heart can rival its fidelity to God. Now is the chalice raised to the altar on high.

Now is the mystic rose, full-blown, plucked for heaven's air. Now is the fragrance of Mary's grace made known to all.

Now above the turrets of the city of eternity rises the tower of David, strong and nobly cast. Now rises the tower of ivory, slender in silhouettes against the blue of the skies of paradise.

Now is the house of gold encased in tender love.

Now is the ark of the covenant lifted to heights of honor that no cedar wood on earth might know, no jeweled casket made by human hands ever receive.

Now is the gate of heaven brought within pearly gates. She through whom grace has entered the world now enters into the reward of grace.

Now is the morning star set in a sky that boasts no greater human splendor nor desires any greater human brilliancy.

Now is the litany ended, for all these things have been. Now is the end, and the beginning is in the end.

Let Mary reign.

GREEN and purple against the August sky the rockets flare. It is the fiesta for our Lady's Assumption.

For weeks the dark-eyed Italian children have been excited. For them, this is one of the big days of the year. Now, running perilously among their almost equally excited elders, they scream with delight at the noise and color of the fireworks. How pleased our Lady must be, they think, as the deep-throated men's voices begin a hymn as traditional as the festival. Must she not smile down at them from her heavenly throne?

Yes, Mary smiles at them. In a world where cold science ignores her, where rampant immorality fears her, where souls go to hell for lack of the grace they will not ask from her, it is good to have this warmhearted loyalty so openly displayed. These are the simple souls whose childlike faith is so like her own. They look up to the heaven where their joyous songs and brilliant rockets ascend. Although they cannot see her there, enthroned in glory after her Assumption, they believe in her celestial queenship.

In this belief there is hope as well as love. She, their Mother, has gone ahead. Will she fail to prepare a place for her devoted children against the time that they will come home to her? All of their lives they have kept this faith in her, from the first prayer learned from their mothers to this act of open belief in her glory before God.

Death cannot frighten such souls. Loving her, they live in joy. Loving her, they will die in peace. Heaven for them is their Mother's home. Let the rockets flare! Let the Queen rejoice!

It was the fourteenth of August. Father Maximilian Kolbe lay, half-propped against the wall of the dismal underground cell where he had been thrust two weeks previous. He did not know what day it was now. He knew only that our Lady had answered his prayer to be the last to die of the ten men sentenced to death by hunger under the brutal Nazi rule in the concentration camp. As punishment for the escape of a prisoner from their block, the ten were chosen at random by the presiding officer. Father Kolbe had not been among those called out.

But he had asked to take the place of one of the victims, a young Pole with a wife and children.

"I am a priest and of no use to you," Father Kolbe had pleaded. "Let me die for him."

So he had gone with the others, driven into the bunker of starvation, as it was called, and his one prayer had been that he might administer to each of his fellow prisoners before death. His Lady, whom he had served so well in forming the Militia of the Immaculate, one of the most successful of the Marian activities in Poland before Nazi occupation, would not deny him this.

He could not pray now, nor think. The habit of years came to his aid, however, and the one picture in his mind was of the Mother of God, his Lady Immaculate. If his lips could have moved, it would have been to say her name.

That it was the Vigil of the Assumption was no mere coincidence. It was the sign of Mary that she loved this son of hers enough to give him as his day of homecoming to her the day of her Assumption, the day of her own homecoming to heaven.

THE strange, gaunt figure of pre-revolution France, Grignon de Montfort, was a powerful force. His preaching reclaimed sinners and made saints for Christ. Whenever he preached, crucifix and rosary in hand, crowds came to hear. With him they labored to erect replicas of Calvary. Following him, they trudged in endless processions and made countless pilgrimages. He was the Xavier of the France of his day.

Yet all this activity is next to nothing when placed beside the influence of a small book he wrote, a little volume destined to be lost in a dusty attic for years. Who could have guessed, as the surging waters of the revolution swept over Paris, that hidden in an old trunk lay the secret of peace?

⋟ 66 ⋞
OUR LADY
OF THE
SECRET

True Devotion to Mary might have been written in the holy man's blood, so sincere it is, so compact, so strong in faith and vivid in love. Like the Master he served, St. Louis de Montfort speaks as one having authority.

The secret of Mary, he says simply, is total gift. Having given all to her, you will receive all from her — all grace, all peace, all sanctity. A child can understand this. Only a saint can fully practice it.

At the end of his explanation of true devotion to our Lady, he wrote, "He that can take it, let him take it." Obviously he realized that such an absolute gift of self would be for a faithful few. Yet that scattered few could restore all things to Christ through Mary.

That the reign of Jesus may come, let Mary reign.

ARTISTS who choose to work at marble with a chisel risk failure at one stroke. A single false move and the masterpiece is wrecked.

The artist who works with a mold is more secure. Providing his mold is perfect, his success is well-nigh assured. His work is easier, his end product bound to be as he desires.

So it is with holiness. Those who work with the chisel of their own efforts may easily fail. Those who pour the weakness of their human effort into the mold of Mary's love risk nothing. By the humility and confidence of the gesture, they acknowledge her power. Being the Mediatrix of Grace and the Queen of All Saints, she will form them to sanctity gently, quickly, surely.

She who molded Christ can with ease mold other Christs.

But for those who seek to be molded by Mary, there must be the constant care to be docile in her hands. Human nature does not often give to her that exquisite attention that is needed for the perfect formation of saints. However beautiful the mold, that which goes into it must be worthy of a masterpiece. Mary can make worthy that which is worthless, it is true. But she will not usurp the will of man to do so. Only a careful conformity to the will of God, which is always, from the very beginning, the will of Mary, makes it possible for her to bring forth, once again, the other Christ that is called a saint.

Mold of God, Mold of Christ, Maker of Saints — into her skilled hands give all your life. Let her mold you to her form, let her pattern you for God. She will not fail Him or you.

Every work of the Mother of God is a masterpiece.

SATAN's soldiers march across the land, and under the jagged sickle and strong hammer, Christian heroes fall. Before them a slender line holds firm, wavers, retreats, goes underground. It is the Legion of Mary.

Heroism is hidden now, but in what blacked-out recess does her statue stand again upon a small table, beside it the scepter of her reign? Few and battered the veterans grouped about her, saying softly the legion prayers. About them all hover the spirits of their martyrs, the boys and girls, the men and women who have died rather than deny the power and purity of Mary. Their names will be known only on the last day.

But those who remain will, like the persecuted of all ages, cherish her banner and her faith. When the blackness of the cloud of irreligion rolls from the Orient, again will rise the Morning Star of Mary. From the bleak regions of disgrace and outrage will come those who are left of her loyal children, and with them the fruits of their hidden apostolate.

"Unless the grain of wheat, falling into the ground die, itself remaineth alone."

Falling they have died, to self-love, to greed, to ambition. With Mary they have accepted beggary and have lost what the worldly world might give them to be great in its eyes, rich with its wealth. They will not remain alone. After them will rise the legions of real success, multitudes of Christian people to proclaim her name over the earth. Christ wins, for Mary leads. *Maria, duce!*

AWAY in far fields Esau strayed, hunting adventure and the pleasures of the chase. He cared nothing for his home or his mother, save that she had fed his hunger, or for his father, save that he might inherit his lands. His brother Jacob he contemned.

Closer at home this younger brother worked, content to be in the fields near the mother whom he loved with a great love, near the old father whose life was drawing to a close.

Rebecca loved this younger son with a special predilection. For him she desired the patrimony. So when the old man called for meat that he might eat a last meal and bless his elder son, Rebecca urged Jacob to try to win his blessing. Skillfully she planned, faithfully he carried out her directions, and the heritage was his.

The story is repeated daily in the world of spiritual values. The Holy Spirit did not inspire its writing for nothing.

Mary has two types of son — the worldly-minded, intent on gain and pleasure; the spiritual-minded, eager to do God's will through her. To the first she cannot give grace, for he will not stay near her, or listen to her words. He does not truly love God, his Father, but serves for fear of punishment or hope of reward. But Jacob, her son young in his attitude of loving dependence, stays near her, does her least biding with alacrity. To his Father, he will appear as attractive as Esau, because Mary will clothe him with the grace of Christ, and give him the meat of steadfast service of God. When he has done what she bids, Jacob will enter into the heritage of heaven.

BEAUTIFUL in the morning sun is the tree of life which is devotion to Mary. Lifting its green branches into the blue sky, it gives shelter to the birds of the air, and shade to those who rest beneath it from the summer heat. In its thick foliage small animals find refuge from beasts of prey.

It is a sturdy tree, deeply rooted and firm in the storm. Though it may bend before the blasts of temptation, it will never fall until it is transplanted to that paradise at the end of the world where it will shine, jeweled and splendid, in the land of eternity.

Here is the cool shade of Mary's care, the quiet ease of her constant companioning. She speaks in the soft murmur of its leaves, and tells us of God.

Here is the refuge of her mercy. Beasts of evil desire cannot harm those who flee to her sanctuary of dusky boughs high above the earth. She will protect the least of her children in the arms of her love.

Other trees bloom and die. The tree of Mary is always green. Its fruit is always ready at her children's hands. And that fruit is Jesus. He is her first fruit and her only fruit. To her faithful ones she gives Him continually.

Sweet on the mountainside is this tree of life. To those who find it, death holds no terrors. Nothing can harm those who live by her.

"Happy the soul in which Mary, the Tree of Life, is planted; happier the soul in which she has acquired growth and bloom."

"My HEART hath uttered a good word. . . ."

The good word that Mary's heart speaks is multiple.

She speaks the personal word of submission: "Be it done unto me according to Thy word." It is a word that covers every action of her life, every thought of her mind, every beat of her heart. There is not a single instance in the life of Mary that is not governed by this word of acceptance of the will of God.

She speaks the word of jubilation: *"Magnificat!"* In a poem of exultation she praises God, the Mighty One who has done wonders for her and through her. Her triumph is His triumph. Her triumph, in fact, is the triumph of the whole world if it will follow her example and do His will.

She speaks a word of charity: "They have no wine." The thirst of generations for the living God is her concern here as well as the relief of a young couple from social embarrassment. They have not even water, she might have said, these children in the desert of a godless world. But she would ask for more than water — let them have the wine of joy.

She speaks a word of confidence: "Do whatever He tells you." It is a repetition of her own act of abandonment. So simple a program to redeem the world! How she has echoed it since then, in every apparition, in every message to the faithful, hearing world.

Her heart utters a good word indeed. Why will we not listen?

71
SPEAKER
OF THE
GOOD
WORD

SMALL children saw our Lady in Belgium in 1933. To them she said: "I am the Virgin of the Poor." Then she showed them her heart of gold.

That is paradox enough — and promise enough — to confuse all but the little ones of God.

Our Lady herself is poor no longer. Mary of Nazareth, who skimped and saved on the meager income of a village carpenter, is now the Queen of Heaven. All its treasures are hers. If she is the Virgin of the Poor, it is her love for the poor that makes her so.

And her heart of gold? It is not that yellow metal of luxury, the desire of which is the root of evil and has caused most of the world's wars. Like fire, like water, gold is a glorious thing. But when desire for it is uncontrolled, like flames and flood, what havoc it can cause. Millions have died to seize it, even in its raw state, as in the Klondike, but more millions have knelt before gold in the finished work of craftsmen in the cathedrals of the world, content to leave it for the worship of God. Simple men have placed bands of it on the hands of faithful wives, a pledge of their loyalty and their faith in love. Gold can be more than glorious, it can be holy.

Our Lady's heart of gold is a sign to us to seek our riches there. "You that have no money, hasten, buy and eat; come ye, buy without money and without payment wine and milk. Why do you spend your money for that which is not bread, and your labor for that which does not satisfy? Ye hearers, hear me, and buy that which is good, and your soul shall rejoice. . . ."

We are all poor but Mary, the Virgin of the Poor. She will enrich with the golden love of her heart.

RAIN glistens on the roses, crimson and white. Such delicate beauty should not know pain. Yet in the soft moss of foliage lie sheathed small silver knives, thorns untender, thorns not kind.

Even the Mystic Rose of Mary Immaculate must wear its wreath of thorns. That which her Jesus bore on His brow in actual agony, she suffers in her heart.

"Comfort her heart," the Holy Child once begged a holy soul, pointing to the heart of His Mother surrounded by thorns. "Comfort my Mother's pain."

We look at her with anxious eyes.

"Sweet Mother, what can we do?"

Her own eyes are not on us but on her Jesus. Despite our deep concern, we almost smile as we realize what she will say.

"Comfort His Heart, my little ones. Comfort His Sacred Heart."

To comfort both, then — that is our task.

Out of the noise of the unmindful world to make a silence for them with our love.

Out of the war of man with man to seek a peace for them, a haven of many hearts to know and serve and love.

Out of the drear forgetfulness of millions to carve a crypt of memory, a chapel of quiet remembrance for these two gentle hearts.

"Even so, come, Lord Jesus. Come, Mother Mary. Come."

NIGHT after day, day after night, wild rains lashed the village. The sun arose at last upon a dismal morass.

Yet in the square stood one inviolate beauty. The eyes of rescue workers sought it unconsciously upon arrival and marveled. A white statue of our Lady remained unharmed in the general destruction, more lovely in its stately queenship than ever before. Under her heavy stone crown, Mary's regal face bent compassionate upon the scene of woe. Many waters could not quench her love, nor could the floods drown it.

Like that village, many a life is in ruins. There are souls who have suffered heavy storms. Say to them:

"Out of the debris, gather what remains of value. Under her eyes sort out the living from the dead. Let this seeming harm be a help to you, a cleansing flood. Rebuild, and soon, here where she watches. Build as she has built, who stands unscathed.

"What has saved her when all else went down in the churning river? It is the firmness of her charity. It is her love.

"Into the foundation that you lay, set firm the seal of this, the love of Mary. Then make this prayer to her.

" 'My Mother, make me steadfast as you. O Queen of Fair Love, teach me to love with your heart. Then come rain and wind and storm! Many waters cannot quench your love, nor floods drown it.

" 'Reign, pure and immaculate Mother, over the small settlement of my heart. Then will the Sun of Justice rise, after tempests rage, on the vision of your impeccable splendor.' "

WE WATCH them go far out to strange pastures, the lambs we love.

(Lady, Shepherdess, guard them well.)

Through long nights we will weep for those who do not come back to the fold.

(O willful and wayward, why have you fled from her care?)

The ninety and nine are safe within. We love them. We cherish them.

(But this stray lamb on the cold hard rocks — alone and afraid! What will become of him?)

He need not have strayed, it is true. There is no reason to explain such conscious wandering. But the heart has its reasons that reason knows not of. . . .

(Mary, he needs you. Do not care that he is to blame. Hear his piteous cry and find him for us!)

She goes, swift in dark as in day. Staff in hand, heart ruling all, speedful in love. He will hear her soft call through the awful night and reply with answering moan. She will find him. She will lift him with gentle strength and carry him home.

(O Mother of lost ones, we give them to you. To them we cannot go, for our duty is here. And always, always, there will be some who will forget you and us, going their own proud and foolish way. They are too young to be wise. When they lose you, O Lady of Green Pastures, sweet Shepherdess of God, seek them and find them. We trust in your love.)

DEEP rose and purple asters lift lazy heads to the mild breeze. Sunlight is everywhere, not a glare but a warm glow of serenity.

Not yet the finality of harvest upon the land, but only a promise of ultimate end.

Not yet the crisp autumn air presaging winter, but a relaxation from intense and enervating heat in a quiet coolness as of forest dells.

This is the land between extremes. In it the gentle days speak well of Mary.

≫ 76 ≪
CALM OF
SEPTEMBER
DAYS

The goldenrod is hers. Its feathered gold is plumed by her soft touch. Tiny globes of fruit upon mock-orange trees yield to her hand their brilliant clusters. The purpling grapes lean to her, but she does not pluck them. Hers is the harvest of a quiet eye.

She loves these days because they mirror peace, and peace is the constant climate of her heart. Even when her sorrows swept above the citadel of her content in God, the inner castle was unstirred. No storm could penetrate the far reaches of her first consent to what God willed.

Upon the landscape of her life falls this silent sun. Over all the atmosphere is sure victory. Beauty breathes in the mellow air. The busy birds have done with building and need not yet think of flying south. They are tranquil among the late flowers.

She will walk in this paradise with her God, a woman clad in quietude. No frost will blacken these blossoms that are hers, these hours that are sacred to her name. September is her month of peace.

ANNE smiled at the flower face of her little one sleeping beside her.

Joachim touched the tiny pink hands with wondering fingers and smiled at Anne's happiness.

That there never was a baby like Mary was the thought in both their hearts.

Silent above them all of heaven smiled. Anne and Joachim could not know how right they were. Never in all the ages a baby like to her except her own Son, and He was God.

The Eternal Father smiled on Mary, and knew delight surpassing mere parental pride. She was the first fruit of the Redemption, saved by a preventative grace, the Immaculate Conception.

More than His original creation, Adam, she pleased Him. More than the unfaithful but repentant Eve. In her alone was fullness of grace. In this, she was like Him who was to come, who would do all things well because He did always the things that pleased God.

O happy fault! Creation dims before this new creation. No marvel wrought in the physical world compares, in the eyes of God, to the fragile little girl asleep. On her heartbeat depends the salvation of the world. Bethlehem's Babe will be more powerful. He will be God Incarnate. But only for this little one, there would be no Bethlehem.

Angels cannot sing her glory now, for she is God's secret. Only the Father Himself can celebrate adequately the birthday of His best-beloved. He is the Gardener of the Mystic Rose.

IN EVERY house of silent love our Lady is at home. Down the still halls she walks on soundless sandals, her face hidden by her veil, her hands lost in her great sleeves.

Wherever the night office is chanted, her voice is raised to glorify God, to rejoice in Him. She kneels in contemplation through long hours of prayer.

The cloister garden knows her step, so gentle, among the flowers. She pauses to touch the cobalt velvet of poised butterflies, to watch a whirring hummingbird's bright wings. Fearless as her shadow falls on them, brown rabbits nibble clover undisturbed. Well they sense that no harm will come from her.

A room with boards for bed and floor for chair, the humble fare of bare refectory tables, the stark cross and skull for decoration — none of these is alien to Mary, Queen of Contemplatives, the Beauty of Carmel. Nothing they do is strange to her. This is her life within expressed in deed without.

Wherever our Lady walked, there was her cloister, for she held heaven in her heart. Hers the rough garb, as of Carmelites, hers the poor food, the simple home. Hers the ceaseless prayer.

And for a garden — she might have had the loveliness of the world. But she chose none of it. The heart of God was the cloister garden where she walked. Within its beauty, she found every joy. He was, to her, an everlasting delight.

THERE is a candle on every grave, hundreds of twinkling lights fit to rival the stars. Rough winds forbear to quench them, for it is All Souls' night.

From the monastery church a chant floats forth. Monks join in the office of the dead, remembrance of those who have died in the Lord, a prayer that they might have perpetual light.

Is not this a mother's task — to remember her children? And Mary, the Mother, guards well the brave candle gleam. Even as she sheltered the light of faith in the souls of those whose bones lie here — dust unto dust — so tonight she bids the wind be still.

Uncertain and fearful, how like this the flame of their spirits once flickered and seemed to fail. But in her care, none vanished finally. In their chamber of death the Christ of Viaticum found faith burning brightly. Joined to His eternal light, they will all illumine heaven eternally.

Hasten the day, beloved Mother. Let them not feel the crueler flames of Purgatory, kind though that cruelty be. Cleanse them quickly from dross. Lead them home soon to thee.

Then will there be no need for these tiny torches in the chill November, save to remind others to pray, to follow them in fidelity.

Soon they will blur in the gray of dawn, will scatter like bright leaves strewn lately by the autumn wind, and be gone.

She who remembers so loyally those who love her is Queen of this night. She is Queen of Remembrance, of long-lasting love. She is the Virgin most faithful. She does not forget her own.

It is no marvel that Mary came to the temple when she was three years old. Although like Jesus, she showed the ordinary development of growing children, her soul was aware from the beginning; her intellect and will awaited no awakening.

Anne and Joachim did not question her dedication to God. Whatever pain the loss of her presence in their home might mean, their knowledge of her happiness in the house of God would more than compensate. Precious she was — a real treasure to give to Him who had given her to them.

≥ 80 ≤

LITTLE
LADY
OF THE
PRESENTA-
TION

How carefully Anne dressed her for that day. Joachim lifted her high upon the little donkey as they began their journey to Jerusalem — her golden hair a sheen above her soft blue robe, her feet daintily sandaled, her eager face more beautiful than anything on God's earth.

The temple court was noisy when they entered it, but she seemed not to be aware, nor did she turn for Anne or Joachim to take her in their arms. Threading through the crowd, they came to the place where the other Anna waited, she who cared for the temple girls.

Did she who later recognized Jesus in the arms of Mary not guess now the miracle of grace that came to her that day? No, it was still God's secret. No fanfare, no celebration for her. Only another little one come to serve the Lord. And her parents, after words with Anna, a quiet farewell to Mary, and a few private prayers in the temple proper, went home.

The gray stones greeted her, the halls where prayers and incense rose. God's house was glad that Mary had come. And little Mary smiled up to God, knowing that His heart, too, was glad.

SOME come to the Catholic Worker building in New York and do not notice the statue of Our Lady of Grace in the library. Others see her standing there, silent and pitiful, and wonder at her being in so drab a place, she who is all grace enthroned in a house that entertains the last of humanity from skid row.

They should know better than to wonder at finding the Mother of Jesus here. He was called the friend of publicans and sinners — and He was. He would not shrink from Bowery bums. In His saints, in His sacraments, He lives among them now even as He did in His lifetime.

The pity of Mary is as wide as the pity of her Son. She is too pure to fear contact with sinners.

On nights when there are no more beds and men must sleep on the library floor, the face of Mary watches tenderly over their restless sleep, her statue there a symbol of the love that never ceases to follow their strange wanderings.

If the Church has lost the poor, it is not because of Mary. The golden crowns upon her head, the massive stone cathedrals raised to her, the praise and reverence of millions have not changed the essential motherhood of Mary.

Here she is perfectly at home. Let the derelict come. He must find her waiting for him.

It is for this that our Lady stands among the least of God's children. She is the Mother of the Outcast, the Madonna of the Poor.

≫ 81 ≪
MADONNA
OF THE
BOWERY

81

THE sick child stirred fretfully in the darkness, half-smothered in the fetid air. He wished that Brother Martin would come to his low bed in the tiny hut, almost lost on the fringe of poverty about the great city of Lima in Peru.

How he loved the tall Martin with his jolly black face and skilled surgeon's hands, Martin in his white Dominican habit with its large rosary, Martin with fresh fruit for his slum children and tales of the saints and their Queen. What was it he'd said the last time he came?

"Ask the Queen of Heaven for whatever you need, and she will get it for you."

The honest little boy pondered, small hand tucked beneath wasted cheek, eyes intent on the single patch of sky visible near the open doorway. Did he really need Brother Martin that he should ask her to send him? Did he really need tangerines, the golden fruit he brought?

Steps in the street outside caused him to stifle a cry. It was Martin! He could tell by the soft jangle of his beads. And he had not even prayed to the Queen for him to come. He had just wished!

"Come with me out under the stars," Martin whispered.

Holding the child effortlessly, he paced the cooler air and listened with a smile to the story of the unprayed prayer.

"Did you wish for nothing else, small one?" he asked jestingly.

"The Lady — did she guess the rest?" was the startled reply.

Martin chuckled. "When you go back, look under your pillow. There may be there a golden gift from the Queen of Heaven!"

ABBÉ PIERRE raised nervous hands to his distracted head. Where would he put them on this freezing night? The streets of Paris were sheeted in ice. For weeks the terrible cold had been killing the city poor. And now these three — Up to this point his shelter had housed only single men who were homeless and jobless. Emmaus was for them. But tonight this tragic family must have room.

He looked at them again. The dejected young father holding a sleeping mite of a child. Also pathetically youthful, the pregnant mother huddled beside the small stove in the hallway. He could not put them out. They could not stay here.

In desperation he went to the chapel, the largest room in the old house where every other room had been divided and divided again to make more living space. Genuflecting wearily, he knelt. Before the Virgin and Child above the little altar he prayed: "Tell me what to do with them."

And suddenly it was quite clear.

His men thought him mad. "But the *chapel*, Father!"

Abbé Pierre brushed aside their scruples.

"God does not mind the cold," he told them serenely. "Tonight His little ones are in need."

So quietly he invited the surprised family into the chapel, from which he carried the Blessed Sacrament to the unfinished and frigid attic for the night. The Virgin and Child remained above the altar, remembering Bethlehem. Tonight, at least, there had been room for them.

"THERE must be a revolution of love, an insurrection of charity," said Abbé Pierre. "Men must discover Christ in the least of their brethren."

It is not a new idea. There is none older in Christianity.

And spearheading that revolution from the beginning has been Mary, the Mother of God, who herself went in haste to the hill country to minister to her aging cousin. That was only the first of her "visitations."

In her name, men have begun all manner of charitable ventures. There is not a religious order in the world that is devoted to the care of the poor and despised which does not owe its inception, directly or indirectly, to her, and which does not honor, often under a distinctive title, the Mother of Charity.

❧ 84 ❧
LEADER
OF THE
REVOLU-
TION

She was with the Spanish Order of Mercy ransoming captives from the Moors. She was with Peter Claver in the holds of the slave ships that landed in Columbia, South America. With John of God she cared for the insane, and with Vincent de Paul she combed the city streets for forsaken children to carry home and care for lovingly.

Every land knows her charity. Those who pray before her statue do not need to pray before a statue of the world. The limits of her love cannot be traced; her mercy and pity have no boundaries.

Wherever there is need, that is Mary's country. The revolution of love has already begun. The Mother of God is its leader.

The inhumanity of man to man can be counteracted only by the individual love of man for man. In this, there is no heart like the heart of Mary, who loves each soul as her own child.

THE young white man in the ragged suit gave the ball a final toss.

"Okay, kids," he called to the colored teen-agers with whom he had been playing in Harlem's Friendship House. "Keep it bouncing. I have to take a look at small fry."

Only one little boy paid any attention to his entrance into the basement playroom. "Tom," he whispered, reaching up a scrap of paper, "draw me a picture."

Tom patted the kinky head. "Sure, kid. What kind of picture."

"Picture of Blessed Mother."

A quick look assuring him that all was well on the cub front, Tom sat down on the bench beside the boy.

"Blessed Mother," he mused aloud, his pencil poised, his eyes on the intent face at his elbow. "With the Baby Jesus?"

"No," came quickly with no premeditation. "Just Blessed Mother. Baby Jesus won't be far away."

Tom's pencil sketched a rough portrait of the Mother of God, a youthful Virgin with a flying veil. "That what you want?" he asked good-naturedly.

The child seized the picture with primitive joy, and with a look of warm gratitude, ran off, murmuring to himself in loving tones, "Blessed Mother, Blessed Mother."

Tom looked after him, affection and admiration on his face. In such singlehearted devotion, he thought, lay the secret of sanctity in Harlem. Her black children recognized Mary as their Mother. With that fact firmly grasped, they would be all right.

And he went back to the ball game.

THE convent had burned to the ground and another was being built. In the half-finished chapel the foreman of the construction job, a burly, uneducated man but a superior craftsman, was surprised standing in contemplation before the window above the altar.

It was an Annunciation window, circular and not too large. In it were a standing angel, a kneeling Madonna, her head bowed in consent, and a single lily in a simple floor vase, all done with remarkably chaste art.

The foreman coughed apologetically like a small boy caught in a theft. He seemed to feel his attitude of reverence demanded an explanation. "I like jest to stand here and look at it," he confessed. "Seems as if the angel is always askin' and the girl, she's always answerin' him."

≫ 86 ≪

THE

TIMELESS

MADONNA

In these few words, theology in a workingman's language defined the timelessness of God, His eternal moment. For the angel does always ask, and Mary continuously answers: "Be it done unto me according to Thy word." Whereupon the timeless God becomes man and dwells among us.

Always the window speaks the endless mystery within mystery. The angel's white and gold, the blue of our Lady's cloak, the creamy gracefulness of the lily light the chapel to splendor. Over and over the angel asks. Over and over our Lady answers. And beneath the window, the Eternal Sacrifice of the Mass is offered, presenting in reality what the window can only picture.

God asks — and Christ answers: "Thy will be done." With Christ, Mary answers also. And with both, the faithful all over the world.

THE selflessness of Mary is more than a mirror of God. Through her grace, as through flawless glass, men can see Him as clearly as merely human virtue can show Him. Mary is the window of God.

Thomas Merton traces the analogy:

Because my will is simple as a window
And knows no pride of original earth,
It is my life to die, like glass, like light:
Slain in the strong rays of the bridegroom sun.

Because my love is simple as a window
And knows no shame of original dust. . . .
I vanish into day, and leave no shadow. . . .*

For her to die is life, life for her and for us. Through her sacrifice of self, she gains God. And because she possesses God and is our Mother, she gives Him to us through the grace of which she is the Mediatrix.

It is as if she could not think of herself at all. In no single moment of her life is she concerned for her own peace, her own comfort, her own success. That is the simplicity of which the poet speaks.

Loving God, she loves His children. And in this turning to others than God with love, she in no way diminishes her devotion to Him.

Human hearts are easily divided in loyalty. They are so limited. They cannot love many others at one time.

But the heart of Mary shares the immensity of God. Loving in Him, with His love, she keeps an integrity of affection that centers all in one act of love. For this reason, Mary's love never attracts souls away from God. Looking through the stainless window of her self-annihilation, they see only God.

---

* Thomas Merton, "The Blessed Virgin Mary Compared to a Window," in *A Man in the Divided Sea*, p. 142. Copyright 1946 by New Directions, reprinted by permission of New Directions.

THERE is a little house of God where the statue of our Lady is completely encircled by windows which tell the full story of the Church of Christ.

The cycle begins with a stained-glass Abraham greeting his angel-visitors, a window in delicate but strong coloring, identified only by a Latin quotation from Scripture beneath it. Then one after another, from entrance to sanctuary, stretch windows depicting other Old Testament foreshadowers of Christ: Moses, Samuel, Samson. The last of these is the Presentation of the Child Mary in the Temple. Then begins the life of Christ, this series of windows embracing the sanctuary itself where, near the Tabernacle, stands a statue of Mary, our Lady of Grace.

From the sanctuary to the entrance, on the epistle side, saints important in the life of the Church are represented. There St. Stephen is stoned, St. Thomas talks with the Crucified Christ, St. Mel and St. Brigid plan monasteries in Ireland, and St. Peter Nolasco kneels before his patron, St. Peter the Apostle.

Round this cycle each day travels the sun. Easterly at morning, by high noon it has reached the sanctuary with its greatest dazzle of blazing color making the statue of Mary a rainbow delight. Toward evening the soft glow dies gradually, as if to say: "This is not the end. The Church goes on, constantly renewing the life of Jesus under the eyes of Mary."

Night falls in the chapel, but the sanctuary lamp promises another dawn when the miracle of continuity will be enacted again.

THE Mediterranean was black with Turkish ships. Defeat for the Christian fleet seemed certain. Even the courage of its leader, Don John of Austria, could not change the wind. Steadily it blew against the ship that flew the cross of Christ.

With the faith of ancient Spain, Don John took his rosary in hand and called upon his men to pray. Only a miracle could save them.

Far off, in the home of the Popes, an old man knelt, rosary in hand also. To his call for arms to save Europe from invasion, only one warrior had replied, this young prince now facing disaster. With his own weapons, the Pope fought with him.

And in the chapel he called upon Mary, his Lady of Victory, his beloved Queen of the Rosary, to rescue the fleet. As he prayed, a new vision was given to him. It was as though he looked with her eyes on the world, through that "secret window whence the world looks small and very dear." In her love he saw the battle — and beyond the immediate danger he saw what victory for the Turk would mean. Desolation upon desolation — and souls lost eternally without help of Church or sacraments. The world seemed to him a child that must be snatched from the hands of a cruel destroyer. With a fresh intensity he prayed: "Holy Mary, Mother of God, pray for us sinners NOW. . . ."

Don John lifted his hand once more to test the wind. He sprang into action. Mary had answered their prayer. Its direction had changed. *"Maria!"* he cried exultantly, and led on to victory.

In Rome, the Pope ordered prayers of thanksgiving. For through his window of Mary's love, he saw that she had saved Europe again.

DAME CATHERINE spoke to Fra Nicholas from her anchorhold.

"I have found a new anchorhold for thee. . . . All of its four walls are love, and love dwelleth in its midst."

Her spiritual son replied, "Through one of its windows thou takest and through one thou givest! And one looketh upon God, and the other upon the world."

"Yea," she answered, "but nay, both windows look upon God."

What the ancient anchoress is here describing is an anchorhold that might well do for moderns. To live in a world from which there seems no flight to God is, to many contemplative souls, an empty misery. Is there no hope for a peaceful retirement from the world and its demands without the complete separation of a Trappist or a Carmelite?

There is the anchorhold of the heart of Mary, the love of Mary, the thought of Mary. Love makes its four walls, just as Love is its indweller, and Love is its only window. The love of God and the love of His children made one for Mary. Hers was a single heart.

Life flowed on about the old anchorholds, and often the world wore a path to the door of the holy people who dwelt there, apart but not disinterested in the lives of the children of God about them. Like the Mother of God, these recluses were unselfish enough to make their own the cares of the world and to bear to God the needs of the universe.

"I have found a new anchorhold for thee," our Lady says. "Both of its windows look upon God."

MUCH as St. John loved our Lady, St. Peter had a knowledge of her that John would never acquire.

Out of the night of Good Friday crept a hulk of a man, blind with tears and broken in the thought that he had failed his Master, the Christ, the Son of the Living God. He did not need rebuke. His eyes had met those of Jesus, and in that light had seen his sin, blacker than the night that had fallen upon the earth. He could not use comfort. He had heard the cock crow, and now Jesus was dead.

Peter remembered His look, gentle and pitying, as He had passed through the court of denial. Yes, He had forgiven His first and most trusted Apostle. Peter had no doubt of that generous forgiveness. Were it not for that, he would now hang beside the dead Judas, a suicide on the dark hillside. What Peter needed now was hope.

⪡ 91 ⪢

MOTHER
OF
PENITENTS

And hope none of the Apostles could give him, for they too lacked it. Only one person in the world that Friday night had the hope that Peter craved. And that was Mary, the Mother of Jesus.

Peter had learned to love this quiet-voiced woman with features so like the Master's and a way of making a crude fisherman feel at home in her company. To her he went now. Before this strength, this courage, this self-effacement, Peter knelt, knowing that her forgiveness would match that of Jesus — she would not turn her face from the boaster who had denied her Son. He laid his big hands in hers, as if to say that only her gentle fingers would hold the eleven together now. He made his act of contrition in her hearing, looking up into her face for courage to go on.

First of the popes, and first of penitents, Peter led the Church to the feet of Mary, Our Lady of Hope.

WITH the outbreak of World War I, Pope Pius X died. Into his place stepped a man who took the name of Benedict XV. His was the burden of heartbreak in a world where there was no peace. Men cried to him for peace, and there was no peace.

In May of the year 1917, he issued a ringing appeal to all the bishops of the world for a mighty crusade of prayer to Mary. He said: "Because all . . . graces are distributed by the hands of the most holy Virgin, we wish the petitions of her most afflicted children to be directed with lively confidence, more than ever in this awful hour, to the great Mother of God.

"To Mary, then, who is the Mother of Mercy, and omnipotent by grace, let loving and devout appeal go up from every corner of the earth. . . . Let it bear to her the anguished cry of mothers and wives, the wailing of little ones, the sighs of every generous heart, that her most tender and benign solicitude may be moved and the peace we ask be obtained for our agitated world."

The letter ordering these prayers was written on May 5. Eight days later, at Fatima in Portugal, our Lady appeared to three shepherd children. One of the first things she said to them was to recite the rosary daily for world peace.

This is the unity of heart between the Pontiff and his Queen. To his appeal the whole Catholic world responded. And to their prayers, the Mother of God paid heed. Through the rosary peace came at last to the warring world.

SHE who is Queen of the Missions loved well the Pope who was called the Pope of the Missions.

He was a quiet man, Achille Ratti, who was to become Pope Pius XI. He divided his worldly interest between the Alps and the library. He sought the heights and their daring solitude. He sought the depths of thought and the adventure of mind meeting mind in world literature. Each hobby was a training for devotion to the missions.

His was the vision that saw the universality of the Church's pattern. With the wisdom of the Mother of Wisdom he set out to place that pattern upon a reality far from ideal, with an audacity and confidence that made some of his confreres gasp.

A native clergy he demanded. And he moved everything in Rome to have a native clergy. It was as if he saw the coming cataclysm, when each nation would stand alone against godlessness, and he strained to give each country, however backward, its own priests. Cut off from the rest of the world, how can a nation survive for even one generation without its own sons to offer Mass and administer the sacraments?

While others talked of the union of nations and their close communication, Pope Pius XI prepared for the separation of nations from the heart of Christendom behind curtains of iron and bamboo.

Mary of the Missions carried on the work she inspired. When her Pope of the Missions died, there was a native clergy trained and in action against the day of disaster. The man of mountains and libraries had done her work well.

BEPPO SARTO knew only one Madonna — Our Lady of Cendrole. To her shrine, during his childhood, he had made many pilgrimages with his family. It was an old statue in a tiny chapel lost in the ruins of an old church, but the boy loved it. Before it he prayed often to know his vocation.

When God, through Mary, called him to the priesthood, young Sarto, a stalwart peasant youth, went with wonder to the cathedral at Castelfranco, where the seminary was located. There stood another Madonna, more artistic and sadder. It was under her tender gaze that he was ordained.

All his priestly life she followed him, so that he could say, "I have always had a great devotion to our Blessed Mother, and I have always felt that I grew up under her protection. And now I am going to Venice where at every street corner, on every island, there are monuments to her."

From Venice he went to Rome. Here too he found his Lady, but in a very different way. It was the Mother of Sorrows who walked with him there. The burden of the Papacy which he assumed as Pope Pius X was appalling as war clouds gathered over Europe. Helpless to stop the madness of men bent on destruction, he cried to her, seemingly in vain.

That the outbreak of hostilities hastened his death was apparent. He could not bear the thought of his children murdering each other. And his Lady, to spare him further anguish, took him home to her heaven. He died during the octave of the Assumption, the day of her jubilee in God's house. There he understood her refusal to answer his prayer. There she wiped away all tears from his eyes.

HORROR was expressed by many secular magazines at the extravagance of language in the prayer composed by Pope Pius XII for the Marian year. A new wave of hatred for Catholic "Mariolatry" broke out. Must they be always deifying Mary, some demanded? Was not Christ enough?

Catholics smiled indulgently and continued to say the prayer with love. To them there was nothing extreme in the praises given to Mary by the Holy Father, nor in the titles he used for her. His was the voice of a son talking to his "sweet Mother," and the reiteration of that very phrase gave a tenderness to his words that no royal title could express.

His "sweet Mother" must look with love upon this son of hers who has been called the Marian Pope. Upon him fell the weariness and wild terror of World War II and the subjection of many of his people to atheistic Communism. With a dauntless soul and wise diplomacy he did what was humanly possible. With a holy heart and an enormous love he did more than most humans could do.

It was the thought of his trust in them that nerved his Catholic children to war against enemies of Christ when that warfare was more than a matter of bullets and death. Confident in his prayers for them, his sons went down to ignominy and the worse-then-death which is madness and physical ruin. With a mother's heart he mourned for them. With a mother's heart he prayed for them.

Unceasingly he called for devotion to Mary, but more than his words, his example inspired modern Catholics. If an Age of Mary is at hand, it is largely because of the Marian Pope.

ON THURSDAY, August 9, 1945, a blinding flash split the sky above Nagasaki. A great ball of fire appeared and stretched to a purple column 10,000 feet high and from its top burst a gigantic mushroom. A gray-white cloud rushed down on the city bringing darkness; a colossal wind swept over the roof tops; the whole city became a mass of flames. This was the atom bomb.

Upon this scene, our Lady looked with pain and pity. Knowing that the inscrutable will of God permitted even such sufferings to come to His beloved children, she would not stop it. But that did not mean her Mother's care did not instantly bend to the stricken city, that Nagasaki which was the ancestral seat of Japanese Catholicity where so many of her children cried to her day and night. Out of this torture she must draw peace. Somehow this cloud of suffering must be pierced by the greater fire of love.

⤝ 96 ⤞

OUR LADY

OF THE

BURNING

CLOUD

The Saint of the Atom Bomb, Dr. Paul Nagai, whose wife was buried in the ruins of their home and who himself lived only five years after the explosion, his body gradually wasting away, was surely a ray of that love that Mary inspired. His devotion to Mary was childlike and entire. Her rosary was his constant prayer, and its mysteries formed a large part of the subject matter for his books and water colors. His spiritual attitude toward the bomb had much to do with the spiritualizing of the minds of Japanese in general on that tragic weapon. It was not unusual that death came to Paul Nagai on the first day of May — May Day, Mary Day.

Out of the burning cloud had stretched the hand of his Mother. Out of the same symbol of destruction she reaches down. From the devastation of many may come, through Mary, the resurrection of many.

A WORLD of disintegration held together by the blue of Mary's love — that is what Salvador Dali has painted in his Port Lligat Madonna. Mother of the Eternal Fisherman, she is at home among the symbols of the sea, the shells, the egg, the barren rocks. With the exquisite dignity of the Renaissance Madonnas whom Dali so admires, she sits enthroned, a Lady of Epiphany in that she shows the Christ, a Child within the tabernacle roofed by her upraised hands.

Everything floats in space here to denote spirituality, says Dali, but it has an even greater significance in that it represents the world dissolved by strife and hate. How shall the whole be bound together? The superb art of Dali does it in the picture by a balance and proportion and a subtle magic that is all his own. As in the spiritual world, the unity is a unity of love. The varied but blending blues in his Madonna of Port Lligat read only one way: the love of Mary holds all together to center the Christ she cradles in her own being. This is a beauty that is also a truth few will see and understand.

The Madonna of Dali is the Lady who holds heaven in her heart and who will give it to men of desire. This is the Lady whose love looks down upon the swirling sea of modern life and, with her Christ, yearns to bring it His peace.

In his Madonna, Dali sees salvation. And through her eyes, in his painting of the Christ of St. John of the Cross, he sees where that salvation lies. His Christ curves from His cross over the same sea as is pictured in the Port Lligat Madonna, as though He would wrench free from the rough wood to plunge into its depths to save. Lady of the Sea, Lady of the yearning Christ, save us in His salvation.

≫ 97 ≪
MADONNA
OF
SALVADOR
DALI

WEAVE, weave a crown for our Lady, silver planes, bright birds wheeling high above her shrine. Let the sunlight glance from your wings to the tall Madonna beside the runway. She is your protecting angel. Let her be your Queen.

Wheel, wheel, birds of a blue Mary sky. Cut in the heavens her name. Remember her. She who looks down at her kneeling children will be aware of your knightly gesture. Write her name where all can see. Let all know that she is Queen.

Rush out through the night sky, a streak of luster in the darkness. You who have knelt bareheaded a moment before, at her side, near her altar, carry light in the memory of that face, tender above you. The flight is in her hands; carry on. Queen of night as well as of day, she will be with you.

Her delights are to be among the children of men, wherever they are. The Madonna of the Home is at once Mistress of the Seas and of the Skyroads. No danger alarms her. Out of the terror of the storm she rides triumphant. Down into the swift rage of accident she goes with calm. She whose Son commands the winds and the waves knows no peril but sin.

Weave, silver wings. Wheel, bright birds. Mary watches you. Over the heights above cities she sees you, over long desert stretches. Weave, silver wings, a crown for your queen. And wheel, brilliant birds, write her name in your sky. Hail as your Queen of Flight the Madonna of the Sky.

It is nearly seven o'clock — block rosary time on America's Main Street. Quietly neighbors begin to gather at the appointed house. They enter without knocking or ringing, and converse in relaxed groups, standing about living room and dining room, rosaries in hand.

As the clock strikes seven, instant silence falls. The group, now numbering almost two dozen, circles the shrine of our Lady in the living room. It is a simple affair. Just a little table statue with a vase of flowers and a vigil light burning before it. Young and old, they kneel on the floor while the head of the house leads the prayers.

There is no Hollywood drama about this little scene. For fifteen minutes, neighbors pray together to the Mother of God. Again and again they repeat the Angelic Salutation with the Our Father and the *Gloria*. The mysteries of the life of Jesus and Mary run through their minds to the rhythm of the familiar words.

Even the children are devout, impressed by the seriousness of their usually chattering mothers and business-like fathers. Older brothers and sisters take on a new maturity in the simple ceremony of a common recitation of the rosary in an ordinary home.

Rosary ended, the group disperses as quietly as it came. There are no social festivities. They have prayed to Mary. Now they return to such work or rest as their own families and position demand. They go with our Lady's blessing, our Lady of their Block.

THEY came unexpectedly as the pilgrimage passed through a tiny village. No one could be identified as their owner and they did not seem to be lost. At the feet of the statue of the Madonna they settled, all three of them — soft, white doves at home with Mary.

Day by day, as the pilgrimage drew near its destination, the doves stayed on. They left the statue only for short flights, and never all at once. No minute passed that at least one of them was not at our Lady's feet.

When the procession neared the cathedral where the statue was to be enthroned, much conjecture was made

about the possible action of the doves. Eager eyes watched them as strong arms carried the Madonna to her pedestal in the sanctuary. Softly the doves hovered over, undisturbed by the noisy devotion of the crowd of Latin enthusiasts for our Lady. When the statue was finally set firmly and left free to them once more, the doves returned to their resting place as before.

High Mass began at once. Through all the singing, incensing, and preaching, the birds remained, watchful but not alarmed. Only as the Mass reached its climax at the Consecration did they stir. Then, as if by instinct, they left the statue and flew to the altar. Upon the high crucifix they perched for the rest of the Mass.

Then, with the "Ite, Missa est," with one accord they flew from the church and vanished. The doves of Mary had escorted her to the palace of the King.

Earthly royalty selects eagles for insignia. Mary, Queen of Peace and Mother of the Prince of Peace, selects doves.

Eve leaned wearily against the hope of God's word. Out of the haunting pain of a hundred years, her eyes looked longingly to the East. When would she come, the promise of pity? When would she come whose Seed would grow to final forgiveness?

There had been that morning when the flaming swords drove them from the gates of Eden. Adam turned brokenly without a further look. But she, Eve, had stood, her hand detaining him. Would not God, even now, forgive? And His voice rewarded her forlorn confidence.

There would come a woman, He had said — a woman who would crush the serpent's head through her Seed. And that was all.

101
PROMISE OF GOD

Into the brambled world of painful labor, Adam had led her then. For how many mornings since Eve had lifted her eyes to the eastern sky, praying for her to come who was to come, and for her strong Seed.

Even on that red dawn when Abel fell beneath the hand of his brother, Cain — oh, my sons, my sons! — she had not despaired. This was her own poor seed, tainted with the sin that was hers and Adam's. It was the seed of disobedience and of death.

But Life would come. The Lord God had promised it. From the bright land of morning would step the woman who carried Life. It would be so.

Eve waited through the years. God would not fail her. Somehow, sometime, He would redeem His pledge. The Woman would come.

OVER the hills of Bethlehem lies the quiet charm of two women who refused to desert a family to which they did not, by race, belong.

When the Jewish husband of Ruth, the Moabite woman, died, and his mother wished to return to her own land of Judea, Ruth went with her. Despite the older woman's urging that she remain in Moab, Ruth clung to her and said: "Whithersoever thou shalt go I will go, and where thou shalt dwell I will dwell, and the land that shall receive thee dying in the same also I will die." So they went to Bethlehem, where through marriage with Booz, Ruth became an ancestor of Christ.

When our Lady was conceived free from sin, she was not, strictly speaking, a daughter of Adam and Eve. There was no real need for her to share their punishment. Yet, like the Moabite Ruth, she threw in her lot with Eve, saying in effect, "Thy land shall be my land."

On the hills of Bethlehem Obed was born to Ruth and Booz, Obed who was to father Jesse, who was to father David, whose family became the family of Christ.

On the hills of Bethlehem was born Jesus, the son of God and the son of Mary, of the house and family of David. Because of Him a star shone there to light the whole world. Because of Him, angel songs awakened shepherds to the wonder of God's littleness in Mary's arms.

Loyalty is the key to the story of Ruth.

Loyalty is the key to the story of Mary of Bethlehem.

Their loyalty is the key to the happiness of the world redeemed.

BEAUTY blinded Assuerus, the Xerxes of the Persian empire, to the Jewish ancestry of Esther, his beloved queen. In the loveliness of her face he forgot that she was of a despised race.

But Esther could not forget. Her people were her people, whatever their degradation and danger, and whatever her fortune and high position.

The test of her devotion to them came when the massacre of every Jewish-born subject in the empire was ordered. Now, said her uncle and counselor, Mardochai, was the time for her to save her people.

"Go," he said to her, "plead with the king to withdraw the decree."

Esther protested. She dared not demand audience with Assuerus. To force herself uninvited into his presence was to court death. She must always wait until he sent for her.

There was no time to wait, Mardochai pointed out fiercely. Soon her countrymen would be put to the sword.

Without further word, Esther arrayed herself in her most beautiful robes and went to the king. Because of his love for her, he pardoned her and granted her the salvation of her people.

"The hand of God is uplifted to strike," said Mary, Queen of Heaven, to the children of La Salette.

"Sweet Lady," we say to her like Mardochai, "hold fast that arm lest it fall upon the children who cry to thee. Be thou our Esther. Save us from the savage enemy bent on our destruction. Save us also from the wrath of God. For love of thee, He will forgive. For love of thee, He will forbear to strike."

HIDDEN and devout, Judith lived a quiet life. No one thought of the youthful and attractive widow when disaster struck the city where she dwelt. Who would suspect that such a one might save them from the enemy, Holofernes, and his host now besieging them?

It was Judith herself who offered to deal with the mighty general in his own camp. The desperate leaders accepted this slim chance of victory, and permitted her to go from the city by night, accompanied only by her personal maid.

When Judith returned, it was with the head of the enemy of her people whom she had slain with her own hand. Electrified to action, the besieged fell upon the army camped outside their walls, and in one day conquered them.

Judith retired to her secluded life, asking no thanks and demanding no privileges. She had acted for God and for her people.

Into the scene of the struggle between Satan and man slips an equally unknown figure. Mary of Nazareth, although of royal birth, was hidden and unrecognized among her own. At God's word she ventured to the front of battle. Still in the darkness of obscurity, she fought, singlehanded, with the enemy, vanquishing him. Then she resumed the silent role that she had formerly played.

Courage clad in woman's weakness is part of the paradox of God. Littleness He allows to conquer seeming greatness.

ALL that King David sang in prophecy, our Lady sang in act.

Out of the root of Jesse flowered his song and hers — but her song was Jesus.

What could the shepherd lad of Bethlehem's pastures know of natural and supernatural beauty that she did not know? What melodies from his harp would awaken ecstasies that she had not experienced?

And when he sang of pain and persecution, Mary matched his minor key with her seven peerless sorrows.

Her mysteries swing through the whole of life. There is not a height or depth unsounded by the music of her heart.

Even sin, which never entered her immaculate heart, she learned well from the Passion of her Son and the penitence of her adopted children. She who has seen the Crucifixion of her Jesus needs no lessons in the misery of sin.

David's somber songs of repentance are lightened with hope:

From the depths I cry to Thee, O Lord!
Lord, hear my prayer.
Let Thine ear be attentive to the voice of my supplication.
If Thou, O Lord, markest iniquities,
Lord, who shall stand it?
For with Thee is plenteous redemption. . . .

The word in which David trusted was the Word of God, received through Mary. His hope is her hope. His hope lies in her. It is she, who in her *Magnificat*, will reply to his cry:

He hath received Israel, His servant, being mindful of His mercy,
As He spoke to our father, to Abraham and to his seed forever.

THE unusual life of Charles de Foucauld is most unusual in its ending. In that end is a strong hint of a Mary-heart in the man who called himself "Poor Charles of Jesus."

His profligate youth, like that of St. Augustine, can be forgotten in the ardent faith of his maturity. When the voice of God spoke to him in the silent desert places, Charles de Foucauld answered with a generosity that burned clear the misery of his past.

Wearing on his breast the red heart symbolic of the love of Christ, he returned from the African desert to France, his own country, only long enough to be ordained. Then back to the Sahara he went, into a self-imposed exile more rigorous than any a religious community would demand. So relentless was his rule of life that no one could share it with him, although since his death many have adopted his ideals.

His key thought was astonishingly like Mary's. He would not actively proselytize but merely live in the midst of the wild tribes of the desert, poor with their poverty, befriending them when possible, as the poor always help the poor. The good he would do them was the raising of the Host each day at Mass — the constant renewal of the Presence of Jesus among them.

In Mary of Nazareth this hidden Apostolate was perfectly lived. In her was the Presence of Jesus first brought into the desert of the world and its lost people. She had nothing of her own to give — only God. Even in that wealth she knew herself poor. Wearing the red heart of her love, God's most beloved pauper carried the treasure that was Christ.

106
POOR
MARY
OF
JESUS

THE pagan gong sounded on the heavy Egyptian air. The throaty chant of a foreign liturgy struck Mary's ear with a solemn dread. She held her little Jesus close and looked at Joseph's strong face.

His own hand was steady enough on the bridle of the donkey she rode, but his look was sad. Not here the beauty of the worship of the one God, Yahweh. Egypt was to the faithful Jew doubly a land of exile. Here the entire body and soul of a man were far from home.

The gong struck again and nearer. Past the ornate temple the humble trio went. Mary pulled her cloak about the Infant in her arms, as if even the air in this place of jade idols might harm Him.

But her gesture wakened Him, and His eyes opened, smiling up at her with all the unconcerned love and carefree joy of Bethlehem.

Swift relief surged through her soul. Why should she fear for Him who was omnipotent? Or why should she conceal Him who is Life and Light from these people sitting in darkness and the shadow of death?

Joseph's gloom lifted at the sight of her and the smiling Child. For him as for Mary there was but one alarm — the security of the God entrusted to their guardianship. His Providence had been with them thus far. And the arm of God was not shortened, he knew.

He lifted his head with spirit and strode a little more quickly toward the goal they had set for that day's journey. Let pagan gongs sound upon pagan ears. For them there was the laughter of this Child and the assurance of His Presence. Even the road of exile was sweet in the company of Jesus.

FOUR young priests of Maryknoll stood at the boat rail watching the coast of California slip from view and the blue Pacific take over the horizon. Softly, as if to the evening star, they sang *"Ave Maris Stella —* Hail, Star of the Sea."

For one of them at least it was farewell for good to America, and for him most of all the hymn was a dedication to Mary, star of his life's sea.

Father Jerry Donovan was to see that star again, so beautiful in hope this evening, so friendly and so near. On an icy Korean night he would lie, alone and in terrible pain, on a bleak hillside where bandits planned his death, and over him would shine that star, remote and cold.

They did not hate him, the bandits, but had kidnaped him for a ransom that was not forthcoming. Many weeks they had hidden with him in the winter hills, half-starved and frozen with the deadly cold. Father Jerry's feet were piteous to see, mere frozen stumps of frostbitten flesh. He could no longer keep up with them as the hunt closed in. They must get rid of him. They would hang him here, and flee.

Father Jerry did not rebel at their verdict. Physically he was too sick and weary to care. And spiritually, this was among the chances he had taken when he had volunteered for the foreign missions.

No warm glow came over him at the thought of martyrdom, but his eyes sought in the inky sky the single star that meant, to him, Mary. She would be with him. She was with him. And his heart sang *"Ave Maris Stella."*

AMONG the rocks at Montserrat in Spain, our Lady went into hiding from the Saracens of the ninth century. From her place of hiding, shepherds far below at the foot of the mountain heard angelic songs on successive Saturday nights.

Adventuring up the steep ascent, they discovered, enthroned on a ledge in a cavern, a diminutive wooden figure of our Lady and the Holy Child, obviously Oriental in workmanship. Ancient chronicles claim that the figure came from Jerusalem by way of Barcelona and thence to the mountains.

The people of the section made a pilgrimage to bring the statue from its rough cave. *La Morenata,* they called her affectionately, the Little Black Madonna, for the image was only thirty-eight inches high and the wood was black with age. For her they built a special church.

During the thousand years of its veneration, the Lady has often had to go in hiding again. During the days of Napoleon — again in 1835 — most recently in 1939. The monastery at the shrine and its monks suffered much from the Reds in the Spanish Civil War. Through all the bloodshed and vandalism, the little statue was safely hidden away, while triumphant searchers hurled the replica that they thought was our Lady of Montserrat into the flames.

With the return of peace, she emerged once more to receive the prayers and homage of her people. With them she shares not only exile but the perils of the hunted. She is our Lady of the Underground.

"THE land that was desolate and impassable shall be glad: and the wilderness . . . shall bud forth and blossom.

"Strengthen ye the feeble hands and say to the fainthearted: Take courage and fear not. God Himself will come and will save you.

"For waters are broken out in the desert, and a path and a way shall be there, and it shall be called the holy way."

What is this holy way in the desert but Mary, the Mother of God?

All the deserts in the world of the spirit have known her footsteps.

Exiles from heaven seek in vain to find their way to the water places alone and unguided. There is a guide for them from the land beyond the thunders. There is a map to lead back to the homeland of their hearts.

Mirage follows mirage for those who trust not in her. Desperate with that bitter desperation of delayed hope, frustrated by the continual defeat, they are likely to lie down and let the death of the spirit claim their souls.

"Lady of the Desert, find them there, disconsolate and broken on the inhuman sands. Show them the holy way that thou art.

"Then shall their eyes look up to the unwonted beauty that is thy love. Even in the desert of the world shall gush forth for them springs of living water. On either side of the pathway will bloom desert roses, the unspeakable glory of the realization of thy love and of the Love to which thou wilt lead them in the kingdom of God."

110

THERE is a garden where a fountain plays night and day. In it sings perpetual summer. But the gate to the garden is hidden. It is a tiny gate, delicate in rustic beauty.

Find us the gate. Oh, find us the gate.

We would enter the garden wonderful by the gate beautiful. Outside of it there is no joy.

What shall we do to find the gate? Oh, tell us, someone, where to find the way to that small door.

A garden enclosed is a mysterious thing. It may be closed because of its rare beauty. It may be closed because there is in it some dread peril.

❧ 111 ❧

THE

GATE

BEAUTIFUL

But we have heard the singing of the fountain. We have seen the birds and butterflies hover over its wall. We have sensed its peace.

Run, children, you who are small. Find for us the gate of the garden. When we have found it, we can open it with ease. It is such a simple wooden gate to the wonderful garden.

Ah, there, the sweet child, Love, has found the gate. Open it! Open it!

We cannot enter here, you say? But we must! There is no happiness but in the beauteous garden.

Be small? But we are not children.

We must be children? We must grow small?

Only a little child can enter the garden by the gate beautiful.

There is no other way.

The garden of Mary is for those who are little in great love.

It was the first day that the statue of the Virgin was to come to their town and its people were excited with plans to welcome her. No queen could be greeted with greater enthusiasm, they said.

Until the last day of waiting for her, the weather favored their preparations. Then, on the afternoon of her arrival, as if the very founts of the sky were opened, rain poured down. Jags of lightning slit the clouds and thunder cracked continuously.

Stolidly the procession and the watchers stood through the hours, while the storm delayed the Virgin's auto escort until almost six o'clock. Then, as the Angelus began to peal from the church tower, the motor cavalcade swept up the street.

With the final stroke of the bell, the violence of the rain ceased. Through a dismal sky the sun shone brilliantly. And arched over all appeared a perfect rainbow. Clear bands of red, green, orange, blue, and violet stretched overhead as if painted with a broad brush on the luminous gray of the heavens.

Clothes did not dry instantly, as at Fatima, but the spirits of the crowd revived. Into the rain-drenched street they bore their Lady, while the children ran beside her, pointing to the gorgeous sky and gleeful at the splendor of their Mother's passage.

It was her rainbow of promise as it was God's sign of hope. Storms do not daunt the hearts that love her. No rage of the elements can match the wonder of the Mother of God. If she lets her children suffer a little, it is only to surprise them with greater gifts. For each favor denied, she reserves a better blessing. She is the Queen of Undying Hope.

"THE globe in her hands represents the world," explained Sister Catherine Laboure, "the world and France and each individual soul."

Close to her heart our Lady holds the globe in the statue of Mary, Queen of the Universe. Hers is a gesture of offering while yet warmly cherishing.

To give away and yet hold close — is it possible for even Mary to do this?

To give to God what is so loved and still to cherish it warm against her heart is the mystery of Mary's heart. And it is the mystery of the love of all the saints, who loved in perfect chastity and yet loved with an incredible human tenderness all whom God confided to their hearts.

This is a mother's gesture. She lets go the beloved child while holding it forever to her heart.

It is a priestly gesture, in which the consecrated hands lift high bread and wine to God only to consume both in Communion.

It is a divine gesture. For is not God perpetually giving life to all? And yet He holds all life in His hands eternally.

So with our Lady. The globe is the world and France, but it is also the individual soul. For Mary there is only one Child, her Jesus. Him she held and Him she offered — and He is hers forever. With each of the other children He has given her, she included in that one offering, that one cherishing. She gives us to God. She holds us perpetually to her heart.

"AND over all the white wings of a dove," wrote Oscar Wilde about the Annunciation. Gerard Hopkins sees the same symbol as a hope for the preservation of beauty in the world:

. . . But for all that, nature is not spent;
There lives the dearest freshness deep-down things;
And though the last lights off the black West went,
Oh, morning at the brown brink eastward springs —
Because the Holy Ghost over the bent
World broods with warm breast and with ah! bright wings.*

≫ 114 ≪

GIRL
BENEATH
OUTSPREAD
WINGS

The dove is admittedly the Holy Spirit, and artists have painted Mary, our Lady of the Holy Spirit, with a dove hovering over her. The bird is more than a symbol of peace. It is more even than purity. This white bird that spreads his lustrous wings over the head of the maiden of Nazareth is Divine Love. In this unearthly symbol — uplifted, heaven-borne — is made concrete for us the incomprehensible love of God for the virgin soul vowed to Him.

Language breaks down before this intangible reality, and so we call her the Bride of the Spirit, well-knowing that these nuptials are above and beyond us.

He who is the Personification of the Love between God the Father and His Son wholly possesses the soul of Mary, full of grace. That mystery which we cannot comprehend we bow before, adoring.

"Lady of Light, Mary of the Holy Spirit, Spouse of the Dove, pray for us. Let the bright wings spread over thee cover us too in the embrace of Divine Love. In that purity and in that peace enfold the world. Teach us His love in thee."

* Gerard Manley Hopkins, "God's Grandeur," in *Poems of Gerard Manley Hopkins* (Oxford: Oxford University Press, 1948).

ORNATE and wonderfully brilliant in gold and gems, our Lady of Perpetual Help looks still wistful, still sad. Hers is the face of profound sorrow. What is it that saddens her when the Child of her God still rests within her arms? Not yet the Passion. Not yet the Cross.

Why is the Child Himself appealing in the tight grasp He has upon her hand? What causes Him to glance apprehensively over His shoulder away from the shelter of her breast?

There are angels near with warning in their hands — the harsh cross, the cruel instruments of torture. Beyond this day of safety in her arms, the Divine Child sees Calvary. And with His sight, His Mother envisions it too.

Why do they not flee from this wrath to come? Why do they not escape now while there is time? Egypt was sanctuary from Herod. There must be some place of refuge from this disaster impending for so sweet a Mother and so dear a Child.

No, see the little loosened sandal? It is a sign that He accepts the future pain. And that she does not tie again the slackened cords admits her agreement with His will.

"Ought not the Christ have suffered, so to enter into His glory," the Child grown will ask.

Mary echoes His words. Let Calvary come. The little foot is ready now to set out on the Way of the Cross. She has already loosened His sandal.

RISING from the sea before the eyes of Elias a light cloud broke the horizon line. The man on the heights of Carmel uttered a cry of joy and fell upon his knees. This was the response to his prayers for release from deadly drought upon the land. From the blessed rain of this little cloud, now no bigger than man's hand's would come new life.

Blessed indeed this harbinger to that far world. Blessed to all at all times the deeper significance of the light cloud of Carmel.

⚹ 116 ⚹

LIGHT

CLOUD

OF ELIAS

For the cloud is Mary. Small in her beginnings, humble and hidden from the sight of all but God, she would bear the precious burden of God which would renew the life of the spirit. With Elias we watch the delicate beauty of the little white cloud. With him we marvel at its long-desired miracle of grace. And with him we turn in joy and thanksgiving to God who gave us Mary.

It is in this cloud that Carmelites hide even today. The world does not know whence its grace comes to it. Prayers are answered often because a Carmelite has prayed. Final perseverance is won for a sinner despaired of, because a Carmelite has prayed. Christian life flourishes in adverse circumstances because, forgotten in cloisters and behind grills of silence, the sons and daughters of Elias pray through Mary. Austere their lives like her own, theirs too is the beauty of her inner life. She is the hidden rose in their enclosed garden, the treasure guarded in their tower of ivory. From her hands, as from the cloud, rain the blessing they gain for a neglectful world.

ONE thing moved Catherine McAuley to action — the pity of God. Her heart was touched by the misery of the Dublin poor. Poverty of body was equaled, among many of them, by poverty of soul. The youth brought up in the slums were especially susceptible to the loss of the faith that had defied centuries of persecution.

There was, her practical soul pondered, only one remedy. If there might be a group of women who would educate themselves to the works of mercy among these people, some of the corporal and spiritual misery might be lifted. To feed the hungry, to give drink to the thirsty, to clothe the naked, to harbor the harborless — this she planned first. Then, when the needs of the body were cared for, to instruct the ignorant, to counsel the doubtful, to pray for the living and the dead.

For a patroness of this venture, as old as Christ is old, she had not far to look. Our Lady had been Mother to her all her life, especially since her parents' death. The title, Mother of Mercy, had been dear to her when she learned of the ancient Order of Mercy that had ransomed the captives of the Turks, giving not only money for their return to Europe and their families, but often substituting for them, going into harsh captivity in the place of others. And all this in the name of Mary, Queen of Mercy, the Pitiful One.

"Sisters of Mercy" she would call her workers, patterning her life and theirs on our Lady. With her and in her spirit they would perform the works of mercy wherever the Holy Spirit led them.

In a dream the mother of St. Dominic saw, before his birth, a dog running swiftly, carrying in his mouth a burning torch.

This was prophetic of his role as Saint of the rosary. From his mouth would come, the vision seemed to say, a message of fire. Speedily his feet would carry it across the continents, to the outposts of the world. Following him would be preachers and penitents, teachers and cloistered saints. Their torch is truth, and their fire the faith contained in the vehicle of truth, Mary's rosary. In that single devotion are held the seeds of all God's mysteries.

St. Thomas Aquinas would light here his torch of burning words. From its heart, St. Rose of Lima would seize the ardent love which gave her beauty beyond the rose for which she was named.

Intrepid missionaries would be the racing feet of this prophetic dog of dreams. Hyacinth, braving the wrath of Russians and wild Tartars, would bear the image of Mary in his words as well as in his arms, and with her help would walk upon the waters to lead his monks to safer shores.

Dominic, the hound of Mary, runs still his course. The truth he bears so faithfully cannot be lost. In prison camps men make rosaries of dried bread, oddly symbolic of what that prayer may be — nourishment and strength. In the mysteries of the rosary men find the bread of truth fired in the flames of the love of the heart of Mary. This is that eternal truth that will make men free.

Run, swift hound, encircle the world with the fire of truth!

THE white cowl and habit of Cistercians is Mary's livery, they boast. It was she who indicated that she wanted such a garb for the sons of St. Bernard.

Small wonder that she was interested in this man and his monks. It is to them that the medieval ages owe the vast growth of devotion to the Sacred Humanity of Jesus, and, consequently, to Mary, His Mother.

"The Usages of the Cistercians are a Canticle to your glory, Queen of Angels," one of them writes, "and those who live those Usages proclaim your tremendous prerogatives louder than the most exalted sermons. The white cowl of the silent Cistercians has got the gift of tongues, and the flowing folds of that gray wool, full of benediction, are more fluent than the Latin of the great monastic Doctors."

To her they dedicate all their houses: *Notre Dame, Notre Dame,* all over the world. And that Lady of theirs is always a Mother with a Child, as the ancient and medieval artists preferred to paint her, seeing in the tender pose a reminder of her Divine Motherhood and of the universal motherhood that cares for all men.

Their silence praises her and imitates her. She who spoke so seldom, and then in praise of God or in charity to men, gives them the grace of silence. For the sacrifice of speech she gives the power of communication with God.

With her they are silent that they may hear His voice. With her they are eloquent with love that they may reply to Him, speaking inarticulately the words that His heart yearns to hear.

THE Jesuits have been called the light infantry of Christ. As such they travel with lightning speed at a mere word of command. For that they must keep free, unrooted, never "at home."

Therefore their Lady is the Madonna of the Wayside.

They meet her as climbers of the Alps meet snow-covered shrines of Mary, solitary as themselves on the perilous slope, steadfast in the midst of blizzard and avalanche.

They meet her in jungles where their sole reminder of her is the medal worn about the bare, bronzed neck of the runner before them. Lush the tropical foliage and brilliant the birds that flash through colorful flower-filled glades. But it is not hers, the surpassing beauty. Not yet. Not yet.

They meet her in the frozen Arctic, among the men who live in furs. They see her carved in rough totem-pole fashion, with the features of the people among whom they dwell. She is the Madonna of the Snow to the natives there, but to the missionary, his Lady of the Way.

No matter what her features or the nature of her shrine, for the men who travel to far places for the Son of God she is Mother. Paint her as they please, this one characteristic predominates. She is the Mother of all men because she is the Mother of Christ. Black skin or white or yellow or brown — she is the Woman who befriends the children of Him who called Himself the Son of Man. It is her heart that is their home however far they travel. She will be with them on the way. She will lead them in the Way that is Christ.

LITTLE Thérèse had lost her mother. The insidious, slow passage of disease had at last killed the beautiful woman so beloved by her husband and children. None missed her, however, so much as the little girl who was her "queen," whose lustrous curls and sunny disposition had won all hearts to her kingdom.

With the death of her mother, Thérèse became a frightened child. The sunshine vanished under the cloud of a grief too great for her frail physique. The least thing terrified her — the shadow of her father's hat on the wall — a strong wind stirring the garden.

No doctors seem to be able to cure such a malady. Thérèse grew weaker and paler until there was no hope that she might live. Sadly her devoted father and older sisters saw their little flower wilt and look ready to die.

⋈ 121 ⋊
SWEET-
SMILING
MOTHER

Trained in childlike confidence in the Mother of God, her sisters knelt one day at her bedside while she screamed in terror at some slight noise. Their father was not at home, and, unable to comfort the terrified child, the two girls turned to a statue of our Lady beside the bed. Aloud they besought that Mother of Mercy to help Thérèse.

A sudden calm came upon the child as their words penetrated the heavy fear about her. She too looked up at the Madonna.

With awe the girls watched their little sister's face. Quiet and peaceful once more, she smiled at the statue with the old radiance they remembered before her illness.

"Our Lady smiled at me," she told them simply. "She smiled at me so sweetly, and she will make me well. She will be my mother now."

ACCORDING to an old legend, an unskilled novice was told to "Paint a picture of our Lady here on the wall." And she obeyed.

No angel hands guided her as she diligently applied the paint. The result was what might have been expected.

Yet she was tranquil as the day approached for its unveiling. While little art had gone into her work, there was much love for Mary in it, and more trust.

"What I have done to you, Mother," she prayed as she hung up the canvas before the wall in the cloister for the last time, "I have done in obedience. Forgive me, and bless the work."

The beholders gasped at the wall when the canvas was drawn back, and not in horror but in delighted surprise. Our Lady had indeed blessed the faithful novice's work.

Upon the cloister wall was a painting, called, fittingly, *Mater Admirabilis*: Mother most Admirable. There was in it such a delicacy of tint as few artists can achieve. Soft and beautiful, its sunrise colors clothed our Lady in youthful morning as she sat, eyes downcast, hands quietly folded in her lap, her mind and heart obviously lost in the heaven of the Incarnation. She was not an idle maiden, for beside her was a workbasket and a book. Behind her, with the traditional lily, stood a distaff and wool. There was something thronelike in the chair in which she was seated, something queenly in the little footstool upon which her small slipper rested.

This is a Lady stolen from heaven by obedience and simple faith. She is our Lady of Youth — the Model of Prayer — the Daughter of Dawn.

ROSY-CHEEKED Herman Joseph ran through the snow. The way to school was long this morning. He would stop a moment at the church.

Even there the chill on the stones crept through his worn shoes. Impulsively he knelt before the statue of the Mother of God, remote and silent far above his small head.

Would she not get him a pair of new shoes?

She would. No sooner said than done. That evening his peasant mother found an unexpected sum of money beneath a bit of loose flooring in the cottage. Herman Joseph got his new shoes.

The little boy ran eagerly to the church, fleet-footed with gratitude. Standing before the Madonna, he showed her the gift of her love. Words seemed so inadequate a thanks. What could he give her in return for her favor?

The weight of his lunch bag answered him. What had he seen his mother put in it today? A shiny red apple.

He looked up at the statue. She was indeed very far away, this Madonna. But the Child in her arms looked as though He might enjoy the fruit.

"Lady-Mother," Herman Joseph said, standing on tiptoe and reaching up the apple as high as he could, "take this for your Jesus."

The rigid stone arm bent to the boy below and took his gift.

Well satisfied, Herman Joseph ran happily on to school.

Those who came to the church thereafter were amazed to see the queenly statue bending still, and holding in her hand the gift of a grateful child.

⪍ 123 ⪌
OUR LADY
OF THE
APPLE

123

"AND, after all," Ti Marto repeated, not bitterly but sadly, "she died alone. She died alone."

He was wrong.

His little daughter, Jacinta, did not die alone in the big hospital at Lisbon where loyalty to our Lady had brought her. Our Lady had come for her there. And the nurse who came in just after Jacinta died marveled at the smile of peace on the face of the suffering child. Quite obviously, she had not died alone.

There is never a moment when Mary forgets those who love her. It is out of the realm of possibility that her perfect loyalty would forsake or forget a heart dedicated solely to her love.

Jacinta knew that her loneliness was only surface. And her father would learn, as the years went by, that Mary did not fail to remember his little girl.

When the whole story of Fatima was told and the world hearkened to the message of Mary to the three children, one phrase proved that Ti Marto was wrong. Jacinta and Francisco had been promised heaven soon, and Lucia cried out to our Lady, "Must I remain here alone?"

"You will not be alone," our Lady told her. "My Immaculate Heart will be your refuge."

So it was with Jacinta before her death. So it is with Lucia now. So it is with all who love Mary. She is the tower of peace in the midst of war. She is a harbor safe from storm. She is our Mother.

This little child . . . throughout
The ghetto passing, never would forego
To lift his voice, and happily to shout
"O alma redemptoris," both to and fro.

The sweetness of Christ's mother had pierced so
Into his heart that for her grace to pray
He could not stop from singing on his way.*

THIS the Prioress of Chaucer tells, in *The Canterbury Tales*, about St. Hugh of Lincoln, the child-martyr who sang to Mary even after death. As they bore his body along the road to the nearest abbey, his clear voice rang out in song, "O alma redemptoris Mater" — "Dear Mother of our Redeemer."

The words and tune he had learned from an older schoolmate and loved them so that he sang them daily, joyous in the memory of the Mother of God. When cruel enemies of the Christians, enraged by the fervor of the Christian song, killed him, still the child sang.

All who came to the abbey to see the body laid there in state marveled at the fidelity of the little one to his Lady. Finally the abbot asked why he sang on, though dead.

Hugh replied: "So sing I must, indeed, in honor always of that blessed Maid, until some hand has taken away the seed of pearl that here upon my tongue she laid. 'My little child,' she said, 'be not afraid, for I will come for you when they have taken this grain away. You shall not be forsaken.' "

The abbot removed the seed of pearl. Our Lady kept her word and Hugh ceased his earthly song to begin her praises in heaven.

125

DEAR MOTHER OF OUR REDEEMER

* Chaucer, *The Canterbury Tales*, modern English version by Theodore Morrison in *The Portable Chaucer* (New York: The Viking Press, 1954).

"WISDOM has built up seven pillars . . . and on them has set thy throne, O Mary."

Reaching from end to end mightily, from the birth of man until his death, the Wisdom of God comes to the world through Mary.

She is the shell of baptism, the small vessel that holds the redeeming waters.

She is the oil of confirmation and extreme unction, strengthening and healing. Hers the hand that smites the youthful knight, the soldier of Christ, and bids him fight for Christ, his King. Hers is the soothing hand upon the brow of the dying, their consolation, their safe-conduct home.

≫ 126 ≪

THRONE

OF

WISDOM

She is the pity of the confessional.

She is the joy of the bridal couple at every nuptial Mass. The music of her words blessed them. Hers is the confidence of the bridegroom to cherish the woman he loves. Hers is the trust of the bride in his strong faithfulness.

She is the hands of the priest that bears the Eucharistic Jesus. Hers the joyful innocence of first communicants. Hers the jubilee of Corpus Christi crowds. Hers the fidelity of nocturnal adorers. Hers the lonely lamp that burns in deserted churches. Hers the happiness of having God-with-us.

O WISDOM, WHO PROCEEDEST FROM THE MOUTH OF THE MOST HIGH, REACHING MIGHTILY FROM END TO END, AND SWEETLY DISPOSING ALL THINGS, COME AND TEACH US THE WAY OF PRUDENCE.

Out of the bush that flowered in flame, the Lord God spoke to Moses. And we reply:

"O strong and beautiful fire of Love that burned without consuming the heart of the Virgin, show us Thy light. Let us hear from her Thy law.

"O Adonai and leader of the House of Israel, come and with outstretched arm, redeem us.

"From the center of the bush of flame, let us see reach out Thine arm of mercy.

"Justice is the sturdy shrub that will not be destroyed. But in its power let Mercy rise to save Thy people.

"Justice the green bough and leaf. Justice the deep root and creeping tendril. Justice the standing rule against winds of change.

"Mercy the lithe flame, bending over and through and around the tree of Justice.

"Teach us Thy law although we are weak. But when we fail to keep it, let flame Thy merciful love.

"Stretch forth the arm of flame to snatch and save.

"Always the burning of this mercy in the bush of Justice. That is Mary's part. In her heart she keeps the warmth and fire of Jesus which flares but does not consume."

✄ 127 ✄

THE BURNING BUSH

O ADONAI AND LEADER OF THE HOUSE OF ISRAEL, WHO APPEARED TO MOSES IN THE FLAME OF THE BURNING BUSH, AND WHO GAVE THE LAW ON SINAI, COME, AND WITH OUTSTRETCHED ARM, REDEEM US.

MARY is terrible as an army set in battle array only to those who are enemies of Jesus. For His own, she lifts up the divine Child who stands for a banner of the people. And the forces of God move forward.

It is before the "Root of Jesse" that she holds aloft, the kings keep silence — silence of awe, silence of adoration, silence of submission. Silence of awe that One so small could be so great. Silence of adoration before the Son of God. Silence of submission before the will divine which speaks from the reaches of eternity: "This is My Beloved Son. Hear ye Him."

And it is before Him that the Gentiles make supplication. Those who have not known the God of Israel will find Him here in Mary's arms. For them, she is Epiphany.

Because of her insistent prayers, because of her complete and generous acceptance of the office of divine motherhood, the petitions of the ages are answered.

"O come!" they cried, "Deliver us and do not linger!"

Only when she cried "Come!" did the stars stir from their orbits to move toward this celestial night. Only when she was willing herself to come to this meeting of stars and kings and the Godhead could a single grain of sand be moved in that vast desert over which kings and camels would pass. Only because of her do men cry still in prayer, and they are answered. She is herself their prompt reply.

THE entrance to Paradise is Mary. The exit from the prison house of sin is Mary. The power of the King lies a scepter in her hands. For Mary is the door of God.

Into the lock of her answer to the Angel Gabriel turned the key of David. With the words she said, the Son of God opened the prison house and set free the captives there. Through her He led them forth to the liberty of the children of God, the wide freedom of His Father's house.

Through the gates of Mary's love still stream the host of those who hope. No man could open what Jesus Christ has opened, Paradise. Nor can any man shut now the gates of mercy once His might has thrown them wide.

Yet how many sit still, mourning and crying, in the prison house of sin. Strong the walls and stout the doors. Who will set us free?

"O foolish and slow of heart," Christ might say again.

No walls can be too strong, nor doors too stout when into the keyhole of Mary slips the slender golden key of grace.

Over the prison bends the cloud of despair. This is the shadow of death. Suns cannot rise on this sorrow nor eyes lift to see the stars of desire. There is no way to freedom but to turn the key.

O KEY OF DAVID AND SCEPTER OF THE HOUSE OF ISRAEL, WHO OPENS AND NO MAN MAY SHUT, AND SHUTS WHAT NO MAN MAY OPEN, COME, AND BRING OUT OF HIS PRISON HOUSE THE CAPTIVE SITTING IN DARKNESS AND IN THE SHADOW OF DEATH.

WITH her decisive will to God, Mary has hewn out the stone of Christ. She is the shaper of the block, rejected by the builders, but become under God's providence the chief cornerstone.

Round it the dust of the centuries swirls. Shall God make stones out of this dust?

He who can make warriors rise from desert stones will not falter here.

"Settle in the peace of the King, O restless dust. Lie quiet, desire of the Gentiles, for He comes, He who makes all one, both Jew and Gentile.

"Under the eye of Mary, and beneath the wisdom of her regard, become sure stones of Christ.

"Build up, dust become stones, build up the temple of God. Until He has a house, how shall He abide with us?

"Make Him a tabernacle here and then we cry: 'O KING OF THE GENTILES AND THEIR DESIRE, THE CORNERSTONE THAT MAKES BOTH ONE, COME, DELIVER MANKIND, FORMED FROM THE DUST OF THE EARTH!' Will He not come when we have thus summoned Him? Will He not come to stay with us?

"Mother of God, our Mother, plead with us for His coming. Lend us your holy prayer, who first called Him and He came. O EMMANUEL, OUR KING AND LAWGIVER, THE EXPECTATION AND SAVIOUR OF THE GENTILES, COME, AND SAVE US, O LORD OUR GOD."

"WHEN I read in the Gospel that Mary went into the hill country with haste into a city of Juda to perform her charitable office to her cousin Elizabeth," writes a Carmelite nun, "I picture her to myself as she passes — beautiful, calm, majestic, absorbed in communion with the Word of God within her."

This is the life of a contemplative. He carries God with him wherever he goes.

In the cloisters they walk, these God-attentive souls, and in the market place.

St. Benedict Joseph walked with God on all the highways of Europe, mingling with the outcasts of earth and untouched by such contact because he was aware only of the God of Grace within his soul.

St. Joan of Arc led crude soldiers to battle and remained the prayerful girl that had talked with saints in her own home.

St. Francis de Sales walked with God in the social life and its distractions that his position demanded of him.

St. Thomas More brought God into the law court and with him to the bench of judge and chancellor.

St. Xavier Cabrini and St. John Bosco found God in little street urchins because they knew Him first constantly in their own hearts.

These are those who say most worthily to Mary: "You are my Mother. You are my Queen."

These are the children most like her. They best carry out her command at Cana to do what Jesus wants, for He desires only that souls "abide" in His love.

131
OUR LADY
OF THE
HILL
COUNTRY

A BEAM of light gleams above the altar as several hundred male voices begin to sing the *Salve Regina*. It is in the monastery church at Gethsemani in Kentucky. This is the evening prayer of the monks.

As the slow, sweeping rhythm of the Gregorian chant sways through the great church, the light behind the altar expands, lighting up at last the whole stained-glass window depicting the Mother of God.

"Hail, Holy Queen," they sing, "Hail, Mother of Mercy! Hail, our life, our sweetness, our hope!"

It is contemplatives who are singing to her, the Queen of Contemplatives. These are men vowed to silence and to Mary. All their lives, like hers, are spent in loving attention to the God within their souls. From the overflow of that inner life with God, their charity, which is truly love, extends in prayer to the whole world.

"To thee do we cry," their evening hymn continues, "mourning and weeping in this valley of tears. Turn then, most gracious Advocate, thine eyes of mercy toward us, and after this, our exile, show unto us the blessed fruit of thy womb, Jesus."

The prayer is said. The petition is made. Yet there is more. A touching addition attributed to the St. Bernard to whom Cistercians owe their origin. It is a delicate tribute, a child's lingering caress.

"*O clemens, O pia, O dulcis Virgo Maria*: O clement, O loving, O sweet Virgin Mary . . .

"Pray for us, O Holy Mother of God, that we may be made worthy of the promises of Christ."

BETHLEHEM was only the beginning. Each soul who finds the Holy Spirit of God as his guest by baptism might say:

> Lonely sat Love in my house,
> A Stranger under my roof. . . .

Unlike our Lady, who never forgot Him, fickle human minds are drawn from this Divine Intruder — for He is always that, however beloved. This God who comes into the secret places of the heart, this too-loving Stranger.

Every man is an island, John Donne notwithstanding. Alone each comes, and alone he goes. Even marriage is, as Francis Thompson says, "a mere knocking at the doors of union."

God comes where none other can penetrate, He comes, a tongue of flame, a cloud of mist, a brooding dove. We welcome Him, but we are afraid.

Even when we learn to know that Love is God and God is Love, we hesitate. Shall we make this Stranger too much at home? We fear lest "having Him, we must have naught beside."

May the Mother of God show us the folly of our fear.

This is peace disguised, this Stranger. This is Love incognito. This invading God is our home and our heritage. He is our life and, would we but give Him the freedom of our hearts, He is our perfect and unparalleled love.

Love need not sit lonely in our house if Mary, too, is there. She who knows how to love will teach us not to fear, but to trust, so that the Divine Stranger may become the Best Beloved.

A RED star burns over Moscow. It is not the star of the Magi. It is not the star of God.

There is no Lady here. Her icons lie buried, their gold blackened and their brilliance gone.

This is the land of the godless. Why should God's Mother remain here when He has been driven away? You will not find such mummery in the land any more, they tell you. For them there is only one star. And it is not the morning star of Mary, nor the star of the sea.

Under the waters of the revolution went down the love for her that was part of the heart of Holy Russia. Down in some subterranean cavern will lie that treasure until the waters recede. Somewhere in that land lives a devotion that is deathless.

Above the night that covers everything with weariness, a red star burns.

Can there be those who look on it, not with fear, but with love? Are there those who say: "For others, Star, you burn with the red of hate. There is no wisdom in your lurid glare. No sheen of green, no glint of blue for Mary. But for us, you burn with love, poor Star. When all the hate is burned away and you fall, a slight ash on the face of the reawakened earth, from that poor dust God will fashion, as of old, a work of love. And in the sky will shine again the Star of His Mother's love, the sign of His Incarnate Son, the sign of His coming.

"Shine on, Star of Hate. We wait patiently. In God's own time will shine the Star of Love."

BETTER to have an inartistic representation of Mary, advises a learned spiritual guide, than a masterpiece, for then you will be less likely to love it for its own sake rather than for hers.

"Find for us, O Mother of God, the picture of yourself that you desire for us, and paint it on our hearts."

By hundreds and thousands they paint them, Madonnas of all the arts. She is a native of countless countries, a model for every artist, the planned masterpiece of each genius.

Yet none of them creates for more than one individual. Each makes a Lady for his heart alone.

Keep, then, your Madonna's canvas a blank until you yourself can fill in its emptiness. Put in no stroke until you are sure what it will say to you. Then, slowly and carefully, commence the work.

No one can see it but God and Mary. If you have skill with words, with paints, with music, you can give hints of your concept of Mary to the world. If you have genius for friendship or success in love, you may reveal her to your heart's kinsmen. And whether you will or not, some slight trace of her beauty will appear in your own life if her image is there beautiful in your soul.

So well will this portrait of Mary reveal you that God might easily judge you on it. And the Church might canonize you for what this picture reveals to human eyes.

"Find for us, Mother of God, that picture of yourself that you desire for us, and paint it in our hearts."

THAT God has exalted Mary is her first praise.

"Blessed art thou, O Virgin Mary, who didst bear the Lord, the Creator of the world; thou didst give birth to Him who made thee, and remainest a virgin forever."

Because He has so praised her, we raise our voices to honor her, yet not knowing what words to employ for that office.

"O holy and immaculate Virgin, I know not with what praise to extol thee since thou didst bear in thy womb the very One whom the heavens cannot contain."

⚸ 136 ⚸

EXCELLENCE SURPASSING THE STARS

And because of this choice to be God's Virgin Mother, Mary was conceived without sin. This is the gift above all human privileges that she prizes — her never broken friendship with God, her perpetual fidelity to Him, her perfect integrity.

"Thou art all fair, O Virgin Mary, and there is no stain in thee."

We praise His work in her: the jewel of her innocence, the pure robe of her virginity, the crowning glory of her Divine Motherhood. Yet in it all there is something which is her work for Him which should also be admired, the virtues that sprang from her co-operation with His grace. The talents that God gave her Mary multiplied a hundredfold.

"Thy virtues, O Virgin, surpass the stars of heaven in number."

Rejoice, O Virgin Mary!
Rejoice a thousand times!

SUCH excellence as shines in the Mother of God is the reason for her power over the world — the world below, the world above. With energy she works for the spread of the kingdom of God, now openly, now hiddenly, but always.

"Glory be to thee, O empress of the world! Bring us with thee to the joys of heaven."

Not often does Mary work spectacular miracles. Like Jesus, she lets her pity cure diseases and avert disasters. She rescues her beseeching children from worldly ruin time and time again. But when the history of the world is revealed on the last day, it will be in the spiritual world that Mary's power will be most noteworthy.

"Glory be to thee, O treasure house of the Lord's graces! Grant us a share in thy riches."

How often mothers mediate between children in disgrace and irate fathers. Mary is such a mother. That is why she is called the Mother of Mercy.

"Glory be to thee, O Mediatrix between God and man! Through thee may the Almighty be favorable to us."

Enemies to man's salvation she slays with her tremendous power. Human pride that seeks by untruth to change the teachings of Christ she battles with her humility. Satan she crushes beneath her immaculate heel.

"Glory be to thee who destroyest heresies and crushest demons. Be thou our loving guide."

Q<small>UEEN</small> of Excellence she is before God, and Queen of Power before men. But before the little ones who call her Mother, she is Goodness.

When deepest ignominy overcomes them in grievous sin, they fly to her. Immaculate herself, yet she can pity them. There is no child however mired in sin that she would not move heaven and earth to save.

"Glory be to thee, O refuge of sinners! Intercede for us with God."

All the lost of the world seek her aid, but more than any she stoops to lift to her heart those who are orphaned. A homeless child is her first concern — a motherless little one, a child left alone. The maternal heart of Mary cannot bear their pathetic cry.

"Glory be to thee, O Mother of orphans. Render the Almighty favorable to us."

While she would leave the ninety-and-nine to go after the lost sheep, Mary loves her faithful children with fidelity. They are her joy and crown. And for those who love her, Mary is joy.

"Glory be to thee, O joy of the just! Lead us with thee to the joys of heaven."

Joy on earth she is, and joy in heaven. Through the dark way of death, Mary conducts her devoted children home.

"Glory be to thee who are ever ready to assist us in life, and in death. Lead us with thee to the kingdom of heaven."

Rejoice, O Virgin Mary!
Rejoice a thousand times!

Out of the darkness of sin God drew a star and named it Mary. Into the star He breathed a light of purity never to be dimmed. And God laughed with a deep happiness as the star glowed for Him in the heaven of His love.

She was His Morning Star, His sign of dawn to come. From the rays of that pure star, He would weave the light of the Sun who would be Jesus.

Into His ruined garden, God planted a seed of joy. With care He fashioned it, with infinite love. No other plant should be so fair. No other grow so strong and so shapely.

From this joy would flower Jesus, the splendor of the Heart of Mary, the Son of God. Over the world its perfume would be wafted until the joy of God would fill all hearts with love.

Under the shadow of an Angel's wings, God spoke one word and Mary answered. O joy of God! Though men sinned still, here was one perfect soul. Here He might find home and housing. Here He might find warmth and love.

"Thou art the glory of Jerusalem, O Mary. . . . Thou art the honor of thy people!"

But more than all else, she is the joy of God.

Into her house He comes to rest until the star can shine for human hearts to see. Then will be lifted up the flower of Christ, the crown of God's joy.

There will be joy in heaven — and that joy will be Mary. There will be jubilee in the heart of God when all see that Mary is His joy as she is the endless joy of all who enter the kingdom of His eternal love.

"O Immaculate Mother, I renew and ratify today, in thy hands, the vows of my Baptism. . . ."

I give myself anew to God. So long ago the deed was done. So far away. Again I renounce Satan, his pomps and works. Again and forever. I am Christ's. I belong to Wisdom.

Who shall witness this offering? Who shall guarantee its efficacy? Who stands by when vows may be forgotten, when the stress of strife with the world and the flesh and the devil is more than human weakness can fight victoriously?

"To be more faithful to Him than I have ever been before, in the presence of the heavenly court, I choose thee this day for my Mother and Mistress, O Mary! I deliver and consecrate to thee my body and soul, my goods, both interior and exterior, and even the value of all my good actions, past, present and future. . . ."

A total gift to Mary is a total gift to God. She has never kept anything for herself.

In her hands all gifts to God are safe. She is the guardian of grace who was once the guardian of God. She who held Jesus safe in her love will not now lose the souls entrusted to her. What is placed in Mary's hands is safe in Mary's hands.

Therefore I leave to thee, O Mother, "the entire and full right of disposing of me and all that belongs to me without exception according to thy good pleasure for the greater glory of God in time and in eternity. Amen."